Jon's lips moved against Stacey's hair and she lifted her face to meet his eyes.

"You are very, very special," he said softly.

Stacey knew that. And so was he.

He touched her chin with his forefinger; she responded automatically, tilting her head. His lips brushed hers. The touch was amazingly soft, like velvet — a brief, tender gesture of affection. Then, hesitantly, he kissed her lips more firmly, testing experimenting. He lifted his head. His smile was sweet and easy, and it said for both of them what did not need to be put into words. There was pleasure in the moment; there was wonder in simply being together. Had Stacey wanted his embrace to end there, it would have. But neither of them wanted that....

Books by Rebecca Flanders

These books may be available at your local bookseller.

Don't miss any of our special offers. Write to us at the following address for information on our newest releases.

Harlequin Reader Service
P.O. Box 52040, Phoenix, AZ 85072-2040
Canadian address: P.O. Box 2800, Postal Station A,
5170 Yonge St., Willowdale, Ont. M2N 5T5

Daydreams

REBECCA FLANDERS

Harlequin Books

TORONTO • NEW YORK • LONDON
AMSTERDAM • PARIS • SYDNEY • HAMBURG
STOCKHOLM • ATHENS • TOKYO • MILAN

Published December 1984

ISBN 0-373-16083-6

Printed in Canada

Chapter One

Light danced. Sound swelled. Sparks flew upward like startled butterflies and dissolved into the night. A rosy mist settled subtly on the high, clear note of a flute, and through it figures drifted, touching and parting, circling and dipping, weaving the threads of silver sorcery into a web that firmly ensnared fifteen hundred people for the space of two hours and ten minutes.

The ballet was *Earth, Wind and Fire: A Trilogy.* The place was Boston, Massachusetts. But the time was a moment apart, a captured fragment of magic that hung suspended in space, a gossamer bubble that reflected windows on the world. Stacey James floated inside that bubble of fairy-tale fantasy in raptured awe, its very fragility making the moment all the more precious.

Jon Callan, premier danceur, was the axis upon which the suspension of disbelief spun. His fingertips whirled the glittering stardust over the audience, his slightest gesture beckoned it into his spell. Breaths hung on his every jeté and pirouette, hearts ached with the pas de deux. No special lighting effects were necessary to enhance the effect of his presence on stage. Jon Callan was magic.

Josie liked to tease Stacey about the crush she had on the famous dancer. Stacey even teased herself. But somewhere deep within her she supposed she knew that hero worship was one thing, what she felt about Jon Callan was quite another.

Stacey's love of music and all things musical was in her blood, a genetic trait she could not deny had she tried. She was drawn to the theater, to the symphony, to the ballet, and with each of the arts she had developed a very special relationship. She had been exposed to the mystical experience of a Jon Callan performance ten years ago, at the same time the rest of the cultured public had, but it somehow seemed she had discovered him first, and alone.

The young man from Peoria, Illinois, was an artistic phenomenon. For an American danceur to achieve international repute was a wonder in itself, but his success story was even more intriguing. Sprung from very ordinary industrial-class parents whose interest in the arts was limited to a Saturday matinee, he had, through extraordinary talent and sheer determination, risen above the competition to receive an invitation to train with the New York City Ballet at age seventeen. At nineteen he had soloed in *Prometheus*. Stacey, who had happened to be in the city that night while settling some routine matters of her father's estate, was at the performance. It had almost seemed to be fate.

Jon had electrified the stage. His performance dazzled critics and viewers alike, and the next day his name was being linked to Nijinsky, Baryshnikov, all the greats. Stacey left the theater awed and dazed, feeling privileged to have been a part of such a historic event.

For three years Callan was a principal with the New York City Ballet; he spent two more years with American Ballet Theatre and was loaned out to prestigious ballet companies throughout the world. During that time he had reportedly received permanent offers from France, England and—if it could be believed—even Russia. His versatility was even more extraordinary than his talent. He did Broadway shows, movies, even television specials. He was presently touring with the avant-garde troupe, Elements, whose style was a mixture of classical, jazz, and modern dance, with strong emphasis on improvisational techniques. Jon was both choreographer and star performer in the highly acclaimed *Earth, Wind and Fire*.

Stacey was impressed by his talent in much the same way as all those without talent are admiring and envious of those who can bring their secret daydreams to life. But, of course, it was much more than that. Besides a reverent respect for Jon's ability, Stacey was touched by a deep, personal regard for him. He seemed completely immune to the threat of celebrity, dedicating himself completely to his audience. Hounded by the media he resisted all attempts to turn him into a commercial hero, shielding his privacy politely but firmly. He had done one or two television interviews, and about twice a year national magazines did feature articles on his success, but, in fact, very little was known about his personal life. There was a certain amount of integrity involved in refusing to exploit oneself for commercial success, and Stacey thought Callan's humility was genuine. He really could not understand why anyone would be interested in anything about him, once he left the stage. He recognized the fact that his dancing was all he had to offer the public and he gave that his all.

Most women indulged the romantic streak in their souls by idolizing rock stars or Hollywood personalities; it said something distinct about Stacey's discriminating personality that she would choose a dancer. But there were times when it almost seemed that Jon Callan had chosen her, and the bond she felt for him was beyond her control. Little things reinforced that feeling of closeness that was no doubt strictly imaginary, but nonetheless intriguing. In his rare interviews Stacey often found herself guessing what he was going to say before he said it. More often than not he answered a question in exactly the way she would have done, and sometimes he even used her exact words. They thought alike, and that closed the gap between celebrity and commoner very comfortably. She felt as though Jon would be an easy man to know—she felt, in fact, that she already knew him, that they had been friends forever. Yet there was still enough mystique about him to fascinate her. He was touchable, yet untouchable. He was a flesh-and-blood hero, and those were the best kind.

Although Stacey had not missed a televised performance, and she had seen his two movies so many times she knew the dialogue by heart, this was only the second time she had seen him in person. She and Josie had made plans months in advance to drive into Boston for the weekend, do some shopping, and treat themselves to an elegant dinner, then attend the performance. Josie's generous and overindulgent husband was staying with their children, and a weekend away from family and chores was in itself a treat for her. But, for Stacey, the one and only purpose of the trip was to be in the presence, even for so short a time, of Jon Callan.

He was magnificent. The physical command he had over an audience was even more powerful than Stacey remembered. There was no way cathode tubes or celluloid could transmit the brilliant effect of that stunning red-gold hair as it whirled like copper gauze around his head, or capture the incredible height of his leaps and the grace of his landings. Each movement was controlled, yet electric, eloquent, and subtle. The smallest gesture spoke a language of its own, even his facial expressions deepened and enhanced the spell. Jon was the embodiment of the perfection of man— physical beauty, purity of soul, depth of emotion. Like all heroes, he made you believe.

Josie nudged Stacey impatiently as the houselights came on for intermission. "Wake up," she said, grinning, "curtain's down."

Stacey knew she was starry-eyed, but Josie was used to it. Reluctantly she got to her feet to follow the crowd into the lobby. "Wasn't it marvelous?" she breathed.

"Let's hurry," urged Josie, pressing against her back. "Maybe we can get another drink before the crowd gets too bad."

Stacey had no doubt that the glass of champagne she had had before the performance had greatly enhanced the spectacle of the performance, but this was a night for celebrating and she did not limit herself to one. The crowd was already thickening around the bar, but Josie, to whom reticence was an alien word, pushed her way intrepidly to the front, dragging Stacey behind her. Stacey followed, as she always did, shaking her head slightly in amusement over her friend's incredibly aggressive self-confidence.

"Drink it fast," Josie advised, gesturing to an empty divan on the far wall, where they might sit and discuss the first part of the performance.

Stacey made a wry face but took a generous sip anyway. "I'll probably pass out. I think I've had more to drink tonight than I ever have had in my life." Stacey's father had been an alcoholic, and early childhood memories had resulted in her never having acquired a taste for liquor or wine. But this was a special night; she threw caution to the wind.

"And miss the rest of Callan's performance?" Josie teased. "You'd crawl back from the grave to get one more look at that gorgeous body. As a matter of fact," she mused, "so would I."

"Who wouldn't?" replied Stacey, and then turned back toward the center of the room as the two seats for which they had been heading were occupied by another couple. The lobby itself was only an extension of the glamour of the stage. The worn spots in the wine carpeting were completely invisible in the soft chandelier lighting and the brocaded divans and hassocks looked elegant against flocked wallpaper. The murmur of conversation was excited and respectful; the gathering of well-dressed men and women enhanced the atmosphere of refined civility. Stacey loved the ballet.

She gave a sigh of appreciation. "Wouldn't you like to just walk up to Jon Callan and shake his hand? Or send him a dozen roses?" she improvised melodramatically. Josie expected it of her. "Or bow at his feet? Just offer some small token of your appreciation?"

"Like my nude body?" suggested Josie over the rim of her glass, and Stacey feigned shock.

"You're a married woman!"

"But you're not." Josie's apple-green eyes twinkled.

Indulging the fantasy for Josie's sake, Stacey mused, "One of these days I'm going to meet him. When I'm a rich and famous patron of the arts, he'll be wandering the streets in search of a daring and innovative new theater, and just happen to hear my name."

"And you'll sweep him off his feet and carry him to your castle in the clouds, where you will perform a pas de deux every night to an audience of mirrors."

"No," sighed Stacey mournfully, trying very hard to keep a straight face, "by that time he'll probably have a wife, three kids, a girl friend, and a bad drug habit to support."

Both women dissolved into champagne-induced giggles, but Stacey, aware of several turning heads, quickly sobered herself. "Drink it fast," she reminded her friend, "we don't want to miss the curtain."

Josie returned to her champagne, but a speculative sparkle lingered in her eyes. It was a look that should have warned Stacey. "So why don't you?" she inquired.

Stacey took another long swallow of champagne. "Why don't I what?"

"Look," persuaded Josie in a tone Stacey knew was more serious than the words implied, "you'll probably never get this close to him again. Why don't you just go backstage and compliment him on his performance?"

To Josie the suggestion was perfectly reasonable. To Stacey it was both incredible and horrifying—mostly because she knew her friend was not teasing. Josie Nubell was one of those rare people who took life by storm. She was intimidated by nothing; shyness was not an affliction she had ever had to endure. When Josie had a problem with a purchase or a complaint about a product, she went directly to the president of the company, person-to-person, long distance. She wrote numerous letters to editors. She had been known to take on the entire school board single-handed over nothing more significant than crumbling

chalk. When she enjoyed a meal she went directly
to the head chef; when she did not enjoy one, she
didn't lose a moment in telling him so. She had
shaken hands with three American presidents and
numerous also-rans, and once engaged in a three-
minute conversation with Yul Brynner, who hap-
pened to be passing through town on his way to a
summer resort. What had they talked about? Sta-
cey breathlessly wanted to know. Nothing much,
Josie had returned with a shrug. Everyone has to
be somewhere.

Last year Stacey and Josie had combined an an-
nual Special Education Conference in New York
City with a vacation, and had been present at the
opening of a new wing of a museum at which the
mayor of New York was officiating. Josie, who felt
that children were never too young to be exposed
to culture, had allowed her oldest daughter to ac-
company them. The child, however, was less in-
terested in culture than in the free soft drinks that
were served before the ceremony, and in the
midst of the proceedings she could no longer hide
her urgency to answer the call of nature. Josie
made discreet inquiries and received erroneous
directions to the nearest facilities several times,
only to return with a frustrated and increasingly
uncomfortable child each time. Finally, deter-
mined to solve the problem once and for all, she
walked up to the mayor at the end of the cere-
monies, complimented him on his speech, and
asked him for directions to the restrooms. The
mayor was most obliging; Stacey could have sunk
through the floor in mortification. When with

Josie, Stacey lived half in fear, half in amused anticipation of what wild thing she would do next; there certainly never was a dull moment.

Stacey thought it was safest to approach this particular situation with lightness and caution, however, so she retorted, "Right. I'll just walk right up to him and say, 'Hi, you don't know me, but I think you're marvelous'. After which he'll swoon right into my arms and beg my hand in marriage."

"Why not?" returned Josie smoothly, and then her mischievous green eyes took on a dangerously alert light, and she declared, "Better idea. Much, much better." She finished the last of her champagne and swept the strap of Stacey's thin purse off her arm in one motion, snapping open the envelope clasp. She removed a package of notepaper which Stacey had had embossed with her name and address only that afternoon and waved it before her, ordering triumphantly, "Send him a note."

Stacey almost choked on her champagne, and she was not certain whether it was with laughter or incredulity. With her wispy red curls piled on top of her head and her glittering eyes Josie looked puckish and childlike; it was almost impossible not to fall into her game. Three hundred and sixty-four days out of the year these women led very staid and ordinary lives: they held responsible, demanding positions; they coped with housekeeping and family pressures; they tried to maintain that delicate balance between service to others and personal satisfaction, and were not always successful. But this, the three hundred and sixty-fifth day, was a time apart. It was made for self-indulgence, schoolgirlish pranks, flights of fancy, and just having fun. Even sensible Stacey was letting down her guard.

"People do it all the time," Josie insisted reasonably, and her dancing eyes issued a teasing challenge. "Just like sending roses to prima ballerinas. Come on, go with it. What would you write?"

But Stacey knew exactly what she wanted to write, and she met the challenge in Josie's eyes with laughter in her own. She gulped down the rest of her champagne and held out her hand for paper and pen. And there, in the midst of the murmuring voices of a thousand people, the clink of glasses, and the subdued laughter, she let a moment of sincerity overcome her within the limits of the fantasy. Stacey actually let herself imagine in all seriousness that she might give the note to Jon Callan, and she wrote exactly what she would have wanted to say to him if she did.

When Georges Sand first saw Frederic Chopin perform, she sent him an anonymous note that read, simply, "Vous êtes adoré."

A truly liberated woman would have used letterhead stationery.

She thought for a moment, but not too long. In daydreams there were no limits, so she added recklessly but sincerely:

You are one of the few people living today I would sincerely like to meet.

You are adored.

Of course, if she were really going to send the note there would be no need to sign it; her name and address were imprinted on top in lavender ink. So she simply tore it from the pad, folded it in half, and waved it before Josie's face with a satisfied smile.

"You're not going to let me read it?" teased Josie impishly.

Now that the fatal deed was done, Stacey felt rather silly. Genuine sentiments had been committed to that paper with thought and care, and the fact that they would never be read made the entire charade seem foolish. But, maintaining the spirit of the game, she shrugged and returned lightly, "Certainly not. This message is for the eyes of the Great One himself and no other." And Stacey started to tuck the note back into her purse.

"Well, it's never going to get to him if I leave it up to *you*," replied Josie firmly.

Stacey afterward was never quite sure how it happened. Somehow the note was out of her fingers and in Josie's hands, and Stacey was standing dumbly in the center of the lobby, while she watched her friend's small figure make its way purposefully through the crowd.

Even after she had regained her senses several moments later, she could not believe Josie had really done it. She kept telling herself the mischief had gotten out of hand and Josie was only teasing. She knew very well Josie would not see anything amiss at all about sending that impulsively scrawled note backstage. There was no point in hoping her friend's better judgment might prevail. Josie's idea of good judgment was light years away from Stacey's.

Still, Stacey tried to maintain a semblance of composure and a shred of false hope as she breathlessly reached her seat, only seconds before the curtain went up. Josie was already sitting back, absently glancing over the program, and Stacey took her relaxed appearance as a good omen. She couldn't possibly have been serious. Stacey sat beside her friend, smoothed the skirt of her green linen suit, and demanded in a friendly, quite calm tone, "All right. What did you do with it?"

Josie looked at her innocently. "I gave it to the security guard at the stage door. He promised me he would give it personally to Jon Callan."

The feeling that shocked through Stacey was a cross between being punched in the stomach and drinking an entire bottle of cold champagne without stopping for air. She was both giddy and nauseous, cold with dread and hot with embarrassment. "You didn't," she said dully, staring blank-eyed at her friend. "Tell me you didn't."

"Shh," admonished Josie. The curtain was going up.

Fire and light were whirling onstage, but it was nothing compared to the fireworks that were going on inside Stacey. She could not be angry with Josie. Stacey never got angry with anyone. Besides, Josie simply wouldn't understand her reaction. Stacey would never be able to convince her that she had done anything wrong. The woman who had blithely taken the mayor of New York away from a press conference to ask him where the restrooms were would not think twice about sending a complimentary note to a performer she admired. But that was just it: It wasn't Josie's note, it was Stacey's, and Stacey never did anything like that. She never pushed herself forward, never objected noticeably or approved loudly of anything life handed her; content to stay in the background and follow in the shadow of her friend's aggressive personality, Stacey preferred anonymity. Daydreams were one thing; this was quite another.

Stacey resisted the impulse to sink further into her seat when Jon Callan made his first appearance onstage. She tried not to think about his reaction when he read the note. Probably, she assured herself, probably he wouldn't even read it. Probably the security guard wouldn't give it to him. And if he did, so what? Just another anonymous compliment from a faceless admirer. That was when a new wave of burning humiliation hit her and she had to grip the arms of her chair to keep herself from melting into a puddle of mortification right on the floor. Her name, address, and phone number were on that paper. She would never be anonymous to him again.

The last act was acclaimed as the most brilliant of the entire performance. Stacey wished she could have seen it. She wished she could stop feeling as though she were sitting in the reception room of a dentist's office. And she also wished she hadn't drunk quite so much champagne quite so fast, because she had a feeling that it was dulling her perception of the entire matter. She probably should have been a great deal more upset than she was, but her emotions were blurred between mild dread, embarrassment, and the amazingly easy assurance that once she was out of the theater it could all be forgotten. She certainly wished she had the courage to wring her friend's neck.

The curtain calls seemed to last forever. Dutifully Stacey stood and applauded with the rest, and all the time she kept her eyes determinedly focused on anything else but Jon Callan. When he took his separate bows the audience roared, and Stacey felt an inexplicable nervous flush spread over her limbs as she tried to avoid looking at him. As soon as she decently could, she grabbed her purse and scooted out into the aisle.

"What's your rush?" Josie asked, close on her heels. Stacey could hear the teasing note in her voice. "Don't you want to go backstage and pay your compliments to the troupe?"

Stacey stopped dead in her tracks, moving out of the way of the exiting crowd to lean wearily against an aisle seat. "Josie Nubell," she said distinctly, "if you *ever* do anything like that to me again you can consider our long and glorious friendship abruptly ended."

"Why?" Josie defended innocently. "You like a movie, you recommend it to your friends. You enjoy a meal, you compliment the chef. When someone gives you a present, you send a thank-you note. It was a perfectly natural thing to do.''

"It was juvenile," responded Stacey, pushing her way back into the crowd again.

"You really need to learn to assert yourself more, Stace," Josie returned the familiar enjoinder, but she knew better than to push her luck.

And then a masculine voice stopped both women in their tracks. "Miss James?"

With dread coiling in her stomach like a cold fist of shame, Stacey slowly turned. A middle-aged security guard in a tan working uniform was standing behind them, addressing Josie. Josie's eyes lit up like Christmas candles and she whispered excitedly to Stacey, "That's him! That's the one I gave the note to."

Stacey's heart started pounding; her face burned and her hands were cold. She wondered if she would be fortunate enough to have a heart attack right then, and she doubted it. Such things rarely ever happened at a convenient time. Wildly she condemned Josie's carrot-red hair and her eccentric way of dressing—tonight she wore a paisley taffeta skirt and a loudly embroidered shawl—which made her so incredibly easy to spot in a crowd. If only they hadn't been sitting in the second row, if only Josie didn't dress so outrageously, if only they hadn't stayed for the curtain calls, they could have made their escape by now and the nightmare that was about to take place would never have happened. The blood that was rushing through her head dimmed the noise of the crowd, and Stacey's heart was beating so fast and so hard it hurt. She did not know what the security guard wanted, but she knew it wasn't good. She hadn't been this frightened since she was sent to the principal's office when she was eleven years old.

The guard repeated to Josie, "Miss James?" and Stacey started to edge unobtrusively away.

Josie's hand clamped around her wrist, preventing escape. "No," she corrected quickly. Her cheeks were flushed and her eyes bright with excitement. "That is, if it's about the note, I'm the one who gave it to you, but the note was from her." She drew Stacey forward with an unceremonious jerk. "This is Stacey James. She sent the note."

The guard looked only momentarily confused, then he directed himself to Stacey. "Mr. Callan asked me to escort you backstage," he said.

For a moment all Stacey could do was stare at Josie in dumb shock. And Josie took advantage of her senselessness to push her forward as the guard, smiling at her reaction, gestured the way. *No*, Stacey thought dully, not believing it. "No," she said in a very small voice, and balked.

"Don't be silly, Stace!" whispered Josie excitedly, giving her a little shove, "this is your chance. Go on."

"I don't want to go." Stacey whispered back, her eyes wide with shock and embarrassment. "I never wanted to. You—"

"You've wanted to meet him for ten years; you'll never get another chance. Go on!"

Stacey was aware of the puzzled look their whispered conference was drawing from the guard. She was on the verge of making a scene. Stacey James never made a scene. She was starting to panic. It would be unforgivably rude to refuse a special invitation like that. She didn't want to be rude. The guard was waiting, obviously growing impatient. What could Jon Callan want with her, anyway? Darn Josie for sending that note. What was she going to do, what could she say . . . .

She grabbed Josie's hand and gritted, "You're coming with me." Then she smiled weakly at the guard and gestured to him to lead the way.

"Ouch!" Josie squeaked, pulling her hand away. "Your nails! What's the matter with you, Stace? This is the most exciting thing that's ever happened to you. Nothing exciting ever happens to you—you look terrible."

Her friend's radiating enthusiasm bounced off Stacey like sonar waves against a reflective shield. "I don't want to meet him," Stacey said desperately under her breath. "I never wanted to meet him." Only in daydreams. In daydreams heros remained pure and undefiled, and that was the way Stacey preferred Jon Callan. No one except dizzy adolescent groupies really wanted to bring their idols to life, and that was exactly what Stacey felt like at this moment—a groupie. "What will I say? I'll just stand there looking stupid. I can't think of a single thing to say. What could he say to me?

Oh, Josie, how could you do this to me? You know I'm no good at this sort of thing."

"Then it's time you learned," Josie soothed firmly. "You'll be just fine. Say whatever it is you've always wished you could say to him. He's only human, after all; he'll be flattered. He must have been flattered or he wouldn't have answered your note. What did you write, anyway? See, you've always had a way with words. You'll know exactly what to say. He's just a man, for goodness' sake—he's not going to bite you!"

Stacey groaned softly as they entered a musty, dimly-lit concrete corridor and the reassuring sounds of humanity faded to the background. Stagehands and mechanics and a few of the costumed dancers hurried by without giving them a second glance. They mounted three shallow steps and made a turn. Stacey's heart was pounding as though she had just broken the three-minute mile, and her palms were sweating. If she tried to talk would her voice shake? Would she stand there, quivering and sweating like a star-struck teenager? How could Josie do this to her?

A series of dressing room doors stretched before her like unanswered questions. Stacey's mouth was dry. Josie insisted in a whisper beside her, "Why are you so nervous? Just act natural. You're finally going to meet him."

Stacey looked at her in despair. How could Josie understand? People like Jon Callan were meant to be viewed, appreciated, enjoyed—from a distance. "I don't *want* to meet him," she hissed back pleadingly. "I don't want to find out that he has clammy palms and bad breath and a pimple on his chin. I was only—"

But the guard before them stopped so abruptly Stacey almost bumped into him. He swung open a door, and laughter and color spilled out. In one split second Stacey was standing in an empty corridor whispering to her friend, and in the next she was whisked inside and it was too late to panic.

Chapter Two

Six or seven people were crowded into the small dressing room, and it was a cacophony of sound. Cast-off costumes, clinking glasses, cries of "Weren't we *marvelous*?", "Best ever, darling!", laughter, and jokes tangled into a surrealistic backdrop of electric excitement that left Stacey somewhat culture-shocked. The room smelled of sweat, wine, and old shoes. Stage clothed ballerinas and scantily clad men wandered around; there was a lot of hugging and teasing and playful squeals. And in the center of it all was Jon Callan.

He looked as though he had just stepped out of the shower, but he was still dressed in the black tights and leather vest he had worn for the last act. The red hair that had looked so striking on stage was now dulled to a dark copper color and clung wetly to his head. Perspiration dripped from his laughing face, and even the leather vest was stained with it. Someone handed him a towel and he began to mop off his arms and neck, involved in a joking conversation with a blond young man who Stacey assumed was the director. Jon couldn't have been more than six feet from her, and she just looked at him.

Somehow Stacey had expected the effect of that perfect body to be diminished in person. It was not. Michelangelo could have used him as a model when he sculpted "Apollo"; da Vinci surely had him in mind when he had drawn "Anatomy." Of course, his body was no different from that of any male dancer or athlete; regimen demanded that anyone in the profession maintain peak physical efficiency. It was just that Stacey had never been so close to perfection before, and the impact was impossible to ignore.

Bunched biceps and strong shoulder muscles rippled as he drew the towel across his glistening flesh. His neck and shoulders were broader than most men's, containing the strength needed to balance a hundred-pound woman high above his head for moments at a time. The oiled flesh of his arms was laced with prominent blue-veined ridges; his hands were long and gracefully boned. Rawhide lacings crossed a bare chest, accenting distinct breast muscles and a torso that was so spare and well-defined it could have been the first page illustration of the human body from a medical textbook. The damp black tights molded themselves to firm, well-developed buttocks and thighs, outlining muscle-lashed calves and strong ankles. Beneath his costume he wore only a dance-belt and the prominent bulge of his masculinity was something Stacey tried self-consciously to avoid seeing. He had been dressed no differently on stage, but this was quite different. He could have been standing naked before her.

At that moment Callan looked up from some laughing comment he had made to the director, bright, busy eyes scanning the room until they rested on the security guard by Stacey's side. Stacey herself was not so visible, dwarfed as she was by the tall man and the bodies which separated her from Callan, and he called out, "So where's that chick who wanted to meet me?"

At that moment the entire thing seemed utterly ridiculous—her nervousness, her embarrassment, her star-struck awe. She was a twenty-nine year old woman, she had been married, she had been self-supporting for the last seven years; she was a department head and music therapist for a three-county school district; she was part-time nurse, mother, and household engineer. And this was Jon Callan, part-time star, full-time human being. Why had she let herself be so intimidated?

She stepped forward, and the smile that deepened her lips was of genuine, relaxed amusement. "Really, Jonathon," she replied, trying not to laugh, "I'm hardly a chick."

Jon looked at her, and was both embarrassed and surprised by what he saw. Not a chick, indeed. This was a mature young woman, so composed and at ease amid this mayhem that he felt he should apologize for the disorder—that, and the crude comment and his sweaty appearance and his boisterous friends and everything in general. He had not known what to expect. He had never received a note like that before. He got occasional fan mail, mostly related to his movie roles, but he never read it. The ballet was not known for its groupies. He had responded to the note impulsively, because it intrigued him and because nothing like this had ever happened to him before. He was certain he had not expected this.

It would have been impolite to let his eyes wander lower than her neck, but Jon got a brief impression of a cool-green linen suit and white silk blouse—elegant and tasteful. Stacey's hair was auburn and arranged in a natural style that flipped up smoothly just below the line of her shoulders, fluffy bangs touched her eyebrows. Jon liked that. Her face was a perfect oval, minimally made up to enhance a soft, peach-colored complexion. There were faint lines near her eyes and her lips that came from laughing. Her eyes were golden-green. She held her head with an easy, proud air that spoke to him of innate strength and confidence, but the slight tilt to it was friendly and relaxed. The little smile was warmly amused, as though she already understood and forgave him for all the things he felt he should apologize for. Right away he was glad he had sent for her.

His grin was a little sheepish as he answered, "No one has called me Jonathon since my mother did." He moved a step closer to her, sealing a space that excluded the other bodies in the room vying for his attention. Stacey noticed that his color, already flushed with exertion and excitement, seemed to actually deepen a bit as he looked at her, and he did not seem to know what to say next. For a brief moment Jon looked awkward and uneasy in this environment that must have been a second home to him, and then he said quickly, "You're Stacey."

She nodded, knowing that she should have introduced herself sooner and spared him the uncomfortable look that crossed his face on the heels of that inane statement. She atoned by adding easily, "I'm surprised you remembered the name."

That seemed to relax him. "How could I forget anything about a note like that?" He smiled at her, and the tension that had been hovering between them dissolved immediately with the naturalness of that gesture. "That was nice," he said simply. "Thanks."

Stacey felt a warm glow begin deep within her and spread outward. So, it was that easy. Just as Josie had said; it was the most natural thing in the world. A sincere sentiment given and received—and appreciated. She should have known it would be this way. She should have known Jon Callan would accept the gesture in the spirit it was meant, and she was glad she had offered it.

She said, "Hasn't anyone ever told you that before?"

Jon looked a little embarrassed. "No. At least, I don't think so." He laughed nervously. "I don't read reviews or fan mail. They upset my digestion." And then he looked at her in a direct, easily frank, no-nonsense way that she somehow had known would be his style. That was the first time she noticed that his eyes were electric blue. "Why did you want to meet me?" he inquired.

That was a hard one. Even if she had wanted to give a flip answer, Stacey knew that none would serve. It was an honest question, generated by genuine curiosity; it deserved no less than a completely honest answer. But she could hardly say to him, *Because everything about you fascinates me and I want to know more, because sometimes I feel that you are the one person in the world I could really get to know, because I have this strange intuition that we could understand each other.* Her smile might have faltered a bit, but not much, as she answered simply, "Because I admire you. I just wanted to meet you, and talk to you."

Something flickered across his eyes, but Stacey did not have time to tell whether her response was received with annoyance, disappointment, or pleasure, because the blond man had pushed his way between Jon and Stacey and was commanding in gruff tones, "Will you get to the showers before you catch pneumonia?" He grabbed Jon's arm and turned him away, grumbling, "That's all I need right now, isn't it, Callan? You have some burning need to see what I look like in a nervous breakdown or something? How's that knee holding up, anyway?"

Jon broke away from him with a scowl and a curt reply that sent the director on his way again after one more dark look. He turned back to Stacey, looking harried and apologetic. "I do have to change," he said. His quick, darting eyes moved around the room. "This place is a madhouse," he sighed.

Stacey kept her smile in place. "I understand."

And then she didn't know what to say next, not entirely sure she was dismissed. He stood there, his eyes floating over the room and back to her again, as though he, too, was uncertain what came now. An inadequate "It was nice to meet you"? An awkward smile and a quick exit? What?

He rubbed the towel across the back of his neck, looking at her, as though he was stalling for time. The hair under his arms was damp and golden-red. Then he said abruptly, "Listen, do you know where the Black Ox is?"

She nodded, taken aback. "Th-that's where I'm staying."

Jon looked both relieved and suddenly tense. "So am I. We could meet, if you like, in the lounge. For a drink. We could talk then. If you want to," he added, almost anxiously.

One part of Stacey could hardly believe it, another part was not surprised at how human he had turned out to be. He issued the invitation just as any other man would to a woman he had just met—uncertain whether she would accept and even unsure whether he wanted her to, giving her plenty of room to back out, while not making himself sound too eager. Just like any other man. How could she refuse?

"I'd like that," she said.

He smiled, still not entirely sure whether he had wanted her answer to be yes or no. "Great," he said, and he half turned. "In about twenty minutes?" he added over his shoulder, and she nodded.

There was one more moment of awkward uncertainty, then he smiled quickly and turned. Somehow Stacey found the door.

Josie was waiting there in the cool, musty corridor, looking excited and very pleased with herself. Until that moment Stacey had not even noticed that Josie had not followed her inside. Until that moment the utter incredibility of what had just happened to her had gone unnoticed, and now it struck her hard.

"Well?" Josie challenged. The tight smile she gave was both teasing and unbelievably smug. "Did he?"

"Did he what?" returned Stacey blankly.

"Have bad breath?"

Stacey sank back against the wall, trying to resolve the crazy, glittering atmosphere of the room only a doorway away with the cool sobriety of the damp corridor. It had been so easy, so natural—just as she had always imagined it would be, but more. In those few brief moments it almost seemed as though they had established a rapport; they had come very close to actually feeling comfortable with one another. But surely that was her imagination. He might not be quite as untouchable as she had first supposed, but he was still a stranger only being polite to a fan. Fan. Was that how he had seen her? It disappointed her to think that, for her appreciation for him, both as an artist and a person, went much deeper than that. But what else could he have thought?

She tried to remember what silly things she had said to him, and was sure she must have seemed like an empty-headed hero-worshiper.

Had she actually called him Jonathon? She could have groaned out loud at the memory, but at the time, it had rolled off her tongue with natural ease. She always thought of him as Jonathon. When she recalled the stilted way in which she had tried to tell him why she wanted to meet him she writhed inwardly with misery. "Because I admire you." How adolescent.

She could not have been inside the room more than three minutes, Stacey realized now, and surely had not spoken more than two dozen ill-chosen words, but at the time it had seemed as though they were well on their way to spending hours together. Those few moments in his dressing room had seemed to fill the space of an entire evening, but now, with the cold roughness of the concrete wall pressing into her shoulders and the echo of faraway footsteps sounding a military rhythm in her ears, she had to admit, practically, that it was nothing more than what it had seemed: a loyal admirer paying brief respects to an artist, who received the unexpected homage with admirable aplomb. It was just that it had all happened so fast, it was hard to put events in their proper perspective.

The dressing room door opened on noise and light and closed again as someone came out. Jolted back to reality, Stacey grabbed Josie's arm and quickly began walking the other way.

Josie, respecting her friend's sudden agitation, waited until the door marked Exit was clearly in sight to demand, *"Well?"*

Stacey took a deep breath, slowed her steps to a

less frantic pace, and tried to adopt a reasonable, journalistic attitude toward the entire episode. She tried to look at it pragmatically. It was easier than she thought. "He was very nice," she said. "He thanked me for the note."

Josie practically chortled with delight. "What did I tell you?"

"He seemed surprised," mused Stacey growing thoughtful as she pushed open the door onto the still chilly April evening. The sounds of traffic and the flash of neon greeted them; yet, in its own way the city, too, was alive with magic. "Nervous, almost." And she looked at Josie. "Do you know, I don't think anything like that has ever happened to him before."

"Very possible," agreed Josie. "He seems to be a very private person."

Stacey nodded, her mind's eye going over every detail of his appearance in the dressing room, recounting body language and unspoken messages, everything that had gone into making him seem so much larger than life, yet so vulnerable. "I read somewhere that he said the only appropriate place for a spotlight is onstage." And then she frowned. "You don't think I embarrassed him, do you?"

"I don't know." Josie was taking the whole thing very casually. "Did he seem embarrassed?"

"A little, I guess. But not offended."

"There you go."

They waited for the light to change at the corner, then ran across the street to their hotel.

"He asked me to meet him in the lounge for a

drink," Stacey blurted when they were on the sidewalk again, gasping for breath.

Josie grinned, not in the least surprised. "Good for you." She took Stacey's arm and urged her into the hotel lobby.

"He probably didn't mean it," Stacey began quickly. "I mean, there are probably after-theater parties to go to and he was just being polite."

"Did you tell him you would?"

"Well, yes." It all seemed so unlikely now. Back in the dressing room it had been perfectly plausible, a man asking a woman to meet him for a drink, a woman shyly accepting. But, now, surely he was regretting ever having spoken. She certainly wished she had never agreed. Without her having been aware of it, Josie had guided her toward the lounge, and Stacey stood at the entrance, hesitating, squirming inside over the mess she had gotten herself into.

She had had her moment. She had met her idol. She had escaped with dreams untarnished and dignity more or less intact; why should she push her luck? Somehow she had managed to make somewhat intelligent conversation with Jon Callan for the space of three minutes, and the effort had exhausted her. What would they find to talk about over drinks? What had he been thinking of when he invited her? Was it just his way of thanking her for an unexpected compliment, an impulse which, by now, he surely bitterly regretted? He probably wouldn't show up. Of *course* he wouldn't show up. And the best thing for Stacey to do was to go to her room and pretend the last part of their conversation had never occurred.

But of course she couldn't do that. What if he did come? Short of leaving town tonight, there was no way to fade into anonymity again. And even that would not help—he now had her name, address, and phone number, and even though he would probably never use any of them, the very thought that he could would haunt her forever. He knew she was staying here, and it would be terribly embarrassing if they were to bump into one another tomorrow before she left—unlikely as that might also be. Besides, she simply couldn't be rude. She could be stood up, but she would not be the one to do the standing up. Once again she found herself wishing she had never bought tickets for that performance tonight.

"You're coming with me," she said grimly to Josie, emphasizing her words with a little push on her friend's elbow.

Josie needed no encouragement. "Are you kidding? I wouldn't miss this chance for the world!"

Stacey took several deep breaths as they walked into the dark, colonial-style lounge. It was, surprisingly, not very crowded; the atmosphere was subdued and soothing. Stacey tried to ignore the clammy feeling in the pit of her stomach and absolutely refused to give in to the runaway pace her heart was threatening again. She tried to pretend she was doing nothing more than having a relaxing drink after an enjoyable evening at the ballet. In all likelihood that was all she was doing. Jon Callan did not want to see her again. Why should he?

"He's staying at this hotel," Stacey said, for no particular reason, sitting at the bar beside Josie.

"Makes sense," agreed Josie. "It's right across the street from the theater." Josie ordered a whiskey sour and Stacey automatically followed suit. She really didn't want anything more to drink. It was hard enough to think as it was.

Determinedly Stacey tried to unravel the reasons Jon might have asked her to meet him. Politeness was uppermost on the list. In which case, the polite thing to do in return would be to thank him and free him from his obligation as soon as he came in. But she had said she wanted to talk to him. He probably assumed from that that she had something of earth-shattering importance to say to him, and she didn't. She began to panic. She couldn't possibly carry the weight of an entire conversation all by herself, when she really didn't have anything at all to say to him.

The drinks were served, and Josie cast her an amused glance as she began to twirl the cherry on its stem with preoccupation. "Haven't you ever been on a blind date before?" Josie teased.

"It's not a date," Stacey snapped. "Besides"—she dropped the cherry back into the glass with a plop—"he probably won't come."

"It certainly is a date," replied Josie. "At least," she qualified reasonably, "it's closer to a date than an execution. You look as though you're waiting for a pardon from the governor."

Stacey sipped her drink and made a face at the bitter taste. If the truth were known, Stacey had not ever been on a blind date before, and that was probably one reason she felt so nervous about making entertaining conversation with a stranger—she had had no experience whatsoever. The rare occasions on which she did go out with men were too casual to be called dates; her escorts were old friends or coworkers, and as likely as not, the entertainment was procured dutch treat. She had not been in a social situation like this since she was in college. No, she had never been in a social situation like this.

"Well, I think you've just reached a milestone in your life," declared Josie in satisfaction. "You've actually asserted yourself, and without a hint of disaster. Didn't I tell you?"

"I didn't exactly do it by myself," Stacey pointed out dryly, and Josie had the good grace to look abashed, even though her eyes twinkled blatantly.

"So you needed a little push," she conceded. "Aren't you glad I did? You did a nice thing for somebody, Stacey; there's nothing wrong with that. And just look what you did for you. You got to meet your lifelong idol and, better than that, you're actually going to get a chance to *know* him. What more could you ask?"

"To go home," replied Stacey glumly.

"Umm, a little more enthusiasm for the woman in the green dress, please," announced Josie in a slightly raised voice, and Stacey looked around furtively, quickly shushing her. Josie grinned. "What is your problem?" she insisted. "Didn't you already tell me he was very nice? So you'll sit and talk for awhile, get to know each other.

What's there to be scared of? He's just another man, for goodness' sake.''

Josie said that as though there were hundreds of other men in Stacey's life. It almost made Stacey want to smile. One of the nicest things about Josie was that she never interfered in Stacey's admittedly arid social life. Blissfully married herself, Josie nobly restrained the impulse to urge her friend in the same direction, and she knew better than anyone that Stacey's experience with members of the opposite sex was embarrassingly limited.

Stacey shrugged lightly, taking another sip of her drink. "Big thrill. He probably eats crackers in bed and leaves the cap off the toothpaste.''

Josie giggled, then stopped with her glass midway to her lips, her eyes focused on a point beyond Stacey's shoulders. "Now's your chance to find out," she said. "Here he comes.''

Chapter Three

Jonathon was wearing a pewter-colored shirt of some silky material, with the collar open and the sleeves turned back; his tight-fitting slacks were of the same color. His hair was once again dried into that glimmering helmet of red-gold that was his trademark, vibrant and satiny as it contoured his face. He walked with a graceful, bouncy step that was as much a part of his distinctive movement as was his performance onstage. It occurred to Stacey that she had never seen him simply walk before, and somehow that seemed rather special. It made her heart speed.

Showered and changed, he looked much more relaxed than he had in the dressing room. The excess nervous energy that had been so noticeable there had faded into only a slight uncertainty, which was obviously no more than the situation deserved. Stacey suddenly realized that Jon must have been just as uneasy about this impulsive meeting as she was, and that he, too, was probably wondering if she would really keep the appointment. She was glad she had.

"Hi," he said when he reached them. "I hope I didn't keep you waiting."

His eyes went from Stacey to Josie in a quick, subtle question, and Stacey said quickly, "No, of course not. This is my friend, Josie Nubell." There, that wasn't so hard. The first sentence was out and the conversation was off to a rocketing start.

Josie extended her hand warmly. "I'm so glad to meet you. The performance was marvelous. Was that your first time at choreography?"

Josie, God bless her. Never at a loss for words, she had easily and naturally erased the awkwardness and engaged Jon in converstion which showed no signs of lagging. Somehow he had eased himself onto the stool beside Josie and they were talking like old friends. Josie asked him if he had ever been to Boston before, and though Stacey thought surely he would resent her ignorance, he responded easily that it was one of his favorite cities. He asked where they were from, and Stacey was drawn into the conversation to describe the little town, a hundred miles away, where she had been born. Stacey should have known better than to worry as long as Josie was along to keep everything going smoothly.

Then the bartender took advantage of a momentary pause in conversation to ask Jon what he wanted. He ordered Perrier with a twist, and then Josie did the most incredible thing. She paid her bill, took up her purse, and stood to leave. Jon, with the old-fashioned manners of a true gentleman, also got to his feet. Stacey only stared at her.

"It's getting a little late for the mother of three," she said brightly, "and I'm driving back tomorrow, so I'll say good night. It was so nice meeting you, Jon," she said, turning to him. "If you ever decide to bring culture to our part of the state, be sure to stop by and say hello."

"That I will," he assured her, his eyes crinkling with unfeigned warmth.

Stacey knew this would be the perfect signal for her to follow Josie's lead and say good night. But she had only taken one or two sips from her drink, and Jon had not even received his yet. The invitation had been for drinks; if she left now, wouldn't that be rude? They had barely spoken to one another. What did he want her to do? She tried desperately to read some hint in Josie's eyes, but Josie was being abnormally obtuse. Josie, in fact, was already calling good night to her over her shoulder as she left the room.

Jon turned to retrieve his drink, but he did not sit down immediately. Stacey was perched awkwardly on her stool, sipping her drink purely to avoid looking at him, knowing she should have left when Josie did. Now he *would* think she had something important to say. He seemed uncertain himself, as though waiting for her to make the first move, wondering what she expected of him. When he spoke it was purely to break the silence. "What are you drinking?"

"Whiskey sour," she responded, and then another insane anxiety occurred to her. Did he think she expected him to pay for her drink? When she did get up the courage to leave, would it be a breach of etiquette for her to pay her own bill? Oh, why had Josie left her alone with this?

But he said only, "Looks good." There was a note of what almost seemed to be envy in his voice.

She made a face. "It's bitter." Then she noticed the glass of mineral water he was absently holding. She wondered why he didn't sit down. "Don't you drink?"

"I can't," Jon responded with a dry twitch of his lips. "At least not during the season or rehearsals, which is all year around. I've drunk enough of this stuff the past ten years"—he lifted his glass—"to float an armada. It starts to lose its taste after a while."

Stacey laughed and was surprised at how relaxed they both seemed to suddenly feel. His smile lingered, and then he said, "Listen, I know you've probably already eaten, but I haven't had dinner yet and I'm starved. Could we go next door to the restaurant? We can take our drinks."

She agreed quickly and gathered up her purse and her drink, and was pleased with the grace with which she got down from the high stool. She said, "I guess you're not supposed to eat before a performance."

"Most of the dancers have a light meal late in the afternoon; I'm usually too wound up to eat. When we're on tour I spend most of my time in a constant state of starvation."

"They say deprivation is good for an artist," Stacey returned lightly. "It hones the senses."

"Could very well be," Jon admitted. "I once

had an instructor who said that a little hunger was what added passion to the dance. I wish she had never told me that; now, whenever I'm onstage all I can think about is T-bone steaks.''

Stacey laughed, and Jon liked that. Now that he was walking a half-step behind her he had his first full-length view of her, and he took advantage of it. As he had first suspected, her figure was soft and round, not voluptuous, but a wonderful contrast to the emaciated women he was used to. She looked healthy, well-developed, normal. The short jacket of her suit did not do more than hint at the curve of her bosom and the indentation of her waist, but there was no doubt that there was a soft woman's figure underneath. Jon had almost forgotten what a woman's breast felt like. Her skirt flared becomingly over a neat swell of hips and brushed against nicely shaped calves. Her ankles were small and delicate. She would never make a dancer. He liked the way she dressed, with modesty and taste. Sometimes, very rarely, he was approached by seductively made-up, garishly dressed women with plunging necklines, who mistakenly thought that because he was a minor celebrity of sorts he was also wealthy. He had been incredibly relieved to discover the author of the sensitive note he had received backstage was not one of those women. Everything about Stacey James spoke of simplicity, honesty, and naturalness, even her name. He felt as though he could relax with her, and he started to put his hand lightly on her back in a spontaneous gesture of the sense of companionship he was beginning to feel.

He changed his mind, though, not certain yet how she would interpret such a movement. It had been a long time since he had been out with a woman and he did not know what to expect.

The hotel restaurant was nearly empty at this hour. The only occupants were a few theatergoers and some members of the ballet troupe. Jon smiled and lifted his hand to them, but deliberately turned the other way when the maitre d' started to lead them to an adjoining table. Stacey was glad.

The table to which the perceptive maitre d' finally escorted them was in a corner, blocked from the view of the other guests by a strategically placed dracaena. When they received the menus, Jon asked her if she would like something to eat, and Stacey, who felt it would be rude of her to make him dine alone—not to mention awkward—ordered pie and coffee. Jon ordered a chef's salad without looking at the menu, and they were alone again.

He folded his hands on the table and looked at her. His expression was relaxed and undemanding. Stacey was not nearly as nervous as she had expected to be. Like everything else, anticipation was worse than the fact, and when she was with him, it was the most automatic thing in the world to want to feel comfortable with him. All of those foolish protests she had made to herself were nothing but falsehoods. She *did* want to get to know him, and she was glad of this opportunity to be with him, and he had never been so much of a hero to her as she had pretended. Once in a lifetime a person was offered an opportunity to explore something really important to her; this was Stacey's chance. She was glad she had not walked away from it.

Jon said, "Sand and Chopin. That was a beautiful love story. I've always wanted to live in that time."

Stacey was not surprised that he should voice one of her own sentiments. "Yes," she agreed. "I don't think things were necessarily simpler then, but they somehow seemed—"

He supplied, as she hesitated, "Purer. Noble hearts and honor to the death. A lot of unrequited love and high melodrama." He grinned a little self-consciously. "The stuff operas and ballets are made of."

"Which is probably why I like the opera and the ballet so much," agreed Stacey. "Of course," she added thoughtfully in a moment, "the story of Sand and Chopin had a rather tragic ending."

"In the true operatic form," Jon pointed out. "Though they loved each other to the end, in their fashion. I think the problem was that both were artists, too obsessed by their talent to commit themselves to anything as mortal as human love. I suppose that's the real tragedy."

"I don't know," Stacey mused. "If they hadn't caused one another so much suffering the world would have been deprived of some great works of art—the immortal 'Funeral March', for example."

He laughed. His eyes caught the sparks of the candle flame when he did. "I never thought of the

'Funeral March' as a love theme before, but I guess that tells it as well as anything else, doesn't it?''

The service was very prompt tonight, and the waiter appeared at that moment to set their dishes before them. Stacey was glad of the interruption because she was certain Jon would have otherwise seen the elation in her eyes. She should have known it would be easy to talk to him. In fact that was the one thing she had sensed about Jon that made him so special. There was an indefinable something about him that made Stacey feel as though they understood one another before they even met. They thought alike. They had common ground between them. That was why she had wanted to meet him.

Jon looked rather disappointed with his salad, and Stacey could not help inquiring, ''Is that all you're having?''

He looked with undisguised longing at her fluffy chocolate pie. ''It's the curse of a dancer. Mineral water and rabbit food. The body is a temple, you know.''

Stacey laughed at the dark look that crossed his face when he said that. ''Come on, it can't be that bad.'' She found it impossible to believe that anyone could maintain a physique as strong and perfect as his on the regimen he had just decried. And for some reason remembering the details of his body as she had last seen it, up close and nearly nude, threatened to make her blush. She quickly took a sip of her hot coffee.

Jon seemed oblivious of her sudden awkwardness and she was glad. "I know some dancers," he admitted, "who can have steak three times a week and bread every day without ever putting on an ounce or losing their concentration. I'm not one of them. I'll be fat by the time I'm forty."

Now she smiled at him. "That I can't believe." And then she frowned a little, curious. "Does what you eat really affect your performance?"

He nodded, picking up his fork. "What I eat, drink, sometimes even what I think. It may look like a glamorous life we lead up there onstage, but it's really a prison of self-discipline." He stabbed viciously at a shred of lettuce for emphasis. "I hate it most when I'm hungry."

She laughed a little because she knew he was dramatizing, and sliced her fork through the thick layers of chocolate and meringue. But then she hesitated, feeling guilty for indulging herself when he was suffering, and she ventured a glance at him.

"Don't let it bother you," he assured her, reading her thoughts. "I've learned to get vicarious pleasure from desserts. I'll just add chocolate pie to the meal I keep promising myself I'm going to blow my diet with someday."

"Which includes?"

"Chili dogs," Jon responded immediately, "French fries, pizza, three different kinds of wine and a bottle of whiskey, Boston cream pie, chocolate cake, pistachio ice cream, cupcakes, cherry pie, apple pie, root beer, a double-decker cheeseburger—"

Stacey pressed her napkin to her lips, her eyes

bubbling over; she choked on laughter. "Please," she entreated, "not while I'm eating!"

The sparkle in Jon's eyes reflected boyish pleasure with her amusement, and his smile lingered as she sobered enough to take another sip of her coffee. It was a good moment in which they laughed together, the turning point that banished all traces of lingering awkwardness and sealed in place the comfortable rapport that had been trying to grow between them. Both recognized the fact, and were grateful for it.

As Jon turned reluctantly back to his salad Stacey said seriously, hesitating only a little, "Do you mind if I ask you a boring question?"

"If you don't mind a boring answer."

"If you hate it so much, why did you become a dancer? And why have you stayed with it so long?"

He smiled thoughtfully, and though Stacey knew he had been asked that question hundreds of times before, he answered it just for her. "I dance because"—his voice was soft and the difficulty he had forming the reply suggested he had never given this particular reply to anyone else before, except perhaps himself—"because it makes me feel as though I have lived before." He could have elaborated, but there was no need. Stacey understood the feeling of continuity and permanence to which he was referring, the sense of being at one with the world and all that had ever lived within it. She felt that way about all music. And there was only the slightest flicker of surprise in his eyes when he looked at her and registered her understanding. "Besides," he added with a negligent smile, "I don't really hate it, you know. I just wish sometimes I could be two people."

He did not offer to explain that, and Stacey did not ask him. After a moment he started eating again and Stacey tried not to feel guilty as she enjoyed her pie. Jon watched her without letting her know that he was doing so, noticing the delicacy of her hands and the prettily shaped, pearly ovals of her nails. The women he danced with all had blunt-cut closely filed nails, at his command. Anything more could be extremely painful, not to mention dangerous, in the intricately balanced steps of a pas de deux. He had never realized before how beautiful elaborately manicured nails could make the hands of a woman look. He followed her movement as she paused to sip her coffee and tuck her hair behind one ear. She wore small gold stud earrings in her pierced lobes — delicate and understated, like the rest of her. He wondered if the silky white material of her blouse was as soft as it looked.

He inquired as she returned her cup to its saucer, "Why did you send the note?"

That caught Stacey a little off guard. She could not elaborate on what she had already said, so she lifted her shoulders lightly, dropping her eyes to her half-empty coffee cup. As honestly as she possibly could, she reiterated, "There aren't too many people in the world you feel as though you'd like to know. For me, you were one of them. I just wanted to meet you."

Jon touched his napkin to his lips to hide a

small smile. His expression was bland. "Despite the rumor that most male dancers are homosexual?"

In the brief moment while Stacey looked at him she tried to analyze how she felt about that. Would it make a difference? She had really never thought about it. And she asked automatically, curiously, "Are you?"

Immediately she realized that was entirely too personal, and she started to blush, desperately searching for a way to take the question back. But his smile only deepened and he answered, "No."

She was ashamed of the small sense of relief he must have seen reflected in her eyes. His sexual preferences were none of her business, that was not why she had wanted to meet him.

Jon rescued what was becoming for her a very awkward moment by demanding easily, "Now, I've got to know who the other people are." There was a friendly twinkle in his eye. "You said I was one of the few people living today you wanted to meet. Who are the others?"

Stacey arched her brows demurely, a smile curving her lips. "I don't think I should tell you that."

"Princes? Kings? Great religious leaders?" he insisted teasingly. "What company am I keeping?"

"Well," Stacey conceded, mischief sparking in her own eyes, "I could tell you this much. One of them is a South American dictator."

He groaned, dragging his hand over his face in mock chagrin. "And another is a notorious war criminal, right?"

She laughed. "You wanted to know." When his eyes sparkled like that he looked like a fun-loving teenager and he made her feel the same way—silly, carefree, open, and ready for adventure. It was such a strange feeling to share a moment like that, such an alien and vulnerable feeling, that it made her suddenly shy. She lowered her eyes briefly and then said, as casually as she could, "I didn't expect you to send for me. As a matter of fact, I didn't even think you would read the note." She did not add that she had not intended to send it in the first place.

His eyes widened with question. "Of course I would read it. I don't get that many messages in the middle of a performance, you know. And after I read it—well, how could I resist? I had to meet the person who'd sent it. It sounded so"—he chose his words carefully, trying to recall exactly how he had felt when he had first read the words—"sincere. I was intrigued. You don't meet too many genuine people in the theater. I had to see if you were really as nice as you sounded." And he smiled at the question she was reluctant to ask. "You are."

He hoped that didn't sound condescending, or patronizing. He wished he could tell her how much it meant to him to be able to spend an evening with a woman like her—a normal, simple, real woman, as far removed from the illusion and the false glitter and the back-stabbing of the theater as night was from day. He wished there were some way to express how relaxed he felt with her, how comfortable she made him feel, as though they had known each other for a long time and he did not have to put on any fronts with her. She probably wouldn't believe it. She would probably think he was coming on to her. He did not want her to think that. He didn't want to do anything to jeopardize the warmth that was beginning to grow between them.

Chapter Four

Obviously, even that small compliment had embarrassed Stacey, and Jon said quickly, "What do you do, Stacey, in the town of Middleton, Massachusetts?"

She responded to the charm of his smile with one of her own. "I'm a music therapist." She was not surprised that confusion should register; few people outside her own field had ever heard of the profession. She explained, "It's an experimental field, using music as part of the therapy for emotionally disturbed and mentally handicapped children. It's really fascinating. We use movement and tone, mood and rhythm to diagnose and treat various symptoms, and the results sometimes are simply unbelievable."

"Like color therapy," he said suddenly, understanding. "You know, where jails use cool blue and green rooms to calm aggressive criminals, and mental hospitals use bright pink or red rooms to stimulate depressed patients—isn't that something like the same thing?"

She nodded, enthused by his interest. "Very

much. There's something about music that speaks to the subconscious, and all we have to do is unravel the messages it sends to communicate with these children in ways that never would be possible otherwise."

"The language of the soul," he said, smiling.

Stacey felt a rush of warmth toward him that was only the result of sharing something special. So few people could relate, even on the shallowest of levels, to her work, but he seemed to understand it with no effort at all. As of course he would. His work was communication through music, just as hers was, and anyone in a similar field would have the same common interest. She must not attach more significance to an imaginary bond than really existed.

"Of course," she went on, disguising her pleasure with an effort, "I've used various tools of special education for the mentally handicapped before—and I still do—but I've got to say music therapy is the most effective. Sometimes it's almost mystical, what happens to the children in my class. It's not that I'm claiming any magical cures or anything like that, but for the hour or so that they're in the program each day, the results are immediate and easy to see—and that's rewarding."

"Do you work in a hospital," Jon inquired, genuinely interested, "or some kind of special school? How did you get the program started?"

Stacey told him about the private school for the emotionally and mentally handicapped, and about her job as a consultant to the public school system, which was just beginning to employ her techniques with behavior-problem students in their own schools.

The waiter came and went, clearing their dishes and refilling her coffee cup, and with a real curiosity, Jon encouraged her to talk, asking intelligent questions, making astute observations, even offering one or two suggestions which they discussed at length, as though they had been working together for years.

The bond of communication is a fragile thing, as delicate as spun glass, difficult to form and capriciously easy to break. What happened between them, Stacey noticed during the course of that simple conversation, was rare and precious. Communication was spun from its finest threads to its strongest rope; the bond that sometimes takes years of understanding and misunderstanding to grow between people was formed between them in a matter of hours. Through the easy exchange of information and opinions, through questions and answers about subjects unrelated to themselves, they revealed more about themselves to one another than detailed autobiographies could have done. They shared thought processes and emotions, body language and listening silences. In an amazingly short period of time, yet so gradually that they hardly noticed it, they learned to read unspoken signals, to respect one another and feel comfortable with one another, as though they had been doing it for years. The door was open, and they felt as though there was nothing they could not say to one another. And, Stacey could tell that

Jon felt as she did—enthusiastic and eager to share more.

"Do you know," Jon said easily, smiling as he leaned back in his chair, "I had a feeling from the minute I read your note that you were a soul mate. It's a lot to presume from a few words, I know, but there was something about it that said you were a music-person too. Not," he explained with a deprecating gesture of his wrist, "like the music people in the theater—all they see is the surface, the motions, and the tempo and the sound of the applause. But you understand the deeper meaning. There's something very special about that. Something real, and rare."

Stacey was touched by his words with a deep warm glow that seemed to flare with the very light that gave her life. Still, her expression as she looked at him was puzzled. "I always envied you," she said, "because you were surrounded every day by people on the same wavelength. Because you could work together with an entire group of people toward the same goal—bringing man's deepest fantasies and most treasured dreams to life. It seemed almost mystical, somehow."

He shook his head briefly, and the slight motion caused the rippling helmet of hair to move with a graceful life of its own before falling again into its natural layers. Stacey had a sudden and almost overwhelming urge to touch that hair, almost to assure herself it was real.

"Don't envy me," he said. "I lead a very sterile existence. All the rumors you've heard about cattiness and throat cutting in the theater are true. There's not one person in this troupe or any other that I would want for a friend, and as far as the mystique goes—it's all as phony as a painted set. My work is satisfying, but that's the only thing about my life I really like. But even that's not as fulfilling as it should be because there's no one I can share it with, not really. Do you know," he told her frankly, on a impulse, "until tonight I never met anyone before whom I could really talk to? Anyone that I even wanted to talk to about things that are important, things that I feel." He shook his head slowly, as if in wonder. "You wouldn't believe how strange it feels to just sit here and talk to you."

Stacey leaned her chin on her fist, and the smile that touched her lips was sweet and soft and abstracted, coming from deep within her. "Yes, I would," she said.

Jon's answering smile brought a brief opening of hearts and a touching of minds, the wonder of understanding that was too awesome to be examined closely or maintained for long. He only knew that he felt buoyed inside, renewed and energized, and desperately eager for more. He asked suddenly, amazed that it had not occurred to him before, "Are you married?"

Stacey shook her head, moving her hand once again to tuck her hair behind her ear. The sputtering candlelight glistened on the small gold earring. "I was," she qualified. "The all-American woman's story. College romance, graduation marriage, and divorce within a year."

"Was it hard being married?" Jon asked curiously.

Though that might have been a strange question to someone else, Stacey was not disconcerted. She gave her answer thoughtfully. "In a lot of ways. I suppose it would have been easier if we had been better matched. Jeff was a dreamer," she explained, "a lot like me on the surface—maybe too much like me. We had a fairy-tale relationship in the truest sense of the word—nothing was real, not even what we felt for each other. Jeff just couldn't quite fit into the real world, where you have to pay your rent on time and work for pay so you can eat, and all of those little things that go into day-to-day living just started to tear down what we thought we had built together. Pretty soon we just couldn't get along at all; we were both terribly unhappy, and very disillusioned."

He nodded. "Maybe that's why Sand and Chopin never got married."

Stacey shrugged, sipping the last of her coffee. "Maybe. Jeff is an accountant now, with a tractor manufacturer in the Midwest."

Jon laughed softly. It was good to be able to sit with Stacey, laughing when he wanted to, talking when he had something to say, being silent when he wanted to, with nothing demanded of him. Knowing that she enjoyed his company just as he enjoyed hers, neither one of them straining to entertain the other.

She said, "What about you? Have you ever been married?" She felt as though she should have known the answer to that question, but, truthfully, she didn't. She knew he was not presently married—at least according to the *Time* magazine feature two weeks ago—but his personal life was so guarded that there was little known about his background offstage.

Again he shook his head, his eyes following the movement of his hand as he swirled the last remaining quarter inch of mineral water in his glass. The turned-back cuff of his pewter-colored shirt fell away from his strong-boned wrist, and Stacey noticed in the dying candlelight that the hair on his arms also appeared to be a very pale copper, with glinting golden highlights. "I think if I were two people," he admitted, "that's one of the things I'd want to do."

The room was empty; the candles on the other tables were extinguished. Busboys were stacking chairs, waiters were counting tips, and the maitre d' was giving Jon and Stacey meaningful looks. Stacey ignored him. A puzzled frown creased her brow as she said, "I don't understand."

Jon looked up, pushing at his hair with a relaxed, graceful motion that shadowed the muscles of his arms as they moved against the gray material. "Maybe I have the same problem Chopin did—you can't commit yourself completely to two great destinies. Loving is an art, just like dancing or composing or writing or painting—they all draw on the same creative energies. And love doesn't just happen—you have to decide to love, just as you decide to get married. You make choices." He shrugged. "I suppose I've made my choices, because the type of life I lead doesn't allow room for split emotions. But I wish it could be different," he admitted honestly, "because I have a very strong suspicion that loving and marrying—the old-fashioned in-sickness-and-in-health, till-death-do-us-part kind—is the ultimate art, the final achievement. You're lucky to have experienced it."

But she hadn't, Stacey realized with a slow wave of sadness. She had experimented like a child with a new toy, only to find what she had thought would last a lifetime was made of plastic and held together by rubber bands. Her experience with loving had been as illusory as the sparkle and canned mist that had flown from the stage tonight. Just more fantasy.

She smiled at him, and if it was a little wan, he understood. "We think alike," she said. "Maybe it's because we have the same birthday."

"Do we?" Jon seemed pleased. "Same year and everything?"

Stacey nodded. "Stellar twins."

He chuckled, his eyes sparkling deep amusement. "Well, that explains a lot, doesn't it?"

"Like?" she retorted, teasing.

She folded her hands under her chin in a portrait pose when she spoke, and her smile was both demure and inviting. Jon's eyes lightened, then deepened strangely when they caught the light in hers. "Like," he responded, and though the tone was frivolous, the sentiment was not, "why I didn't run for cover the minute I read your note. It's pretty intimidating to be adored by a stranger, you know. But the stars must have been smiling down on me tonight because I surely wouldn't have had the courage to answer you if they hadn't been.''

The tilt of her head was innocently alluring, the deepening of her smile soft and vague. Adored. She did adore him, more now that she knew him than she had before. It was far too perfect to be true. "I'm glad you did," she said.

Jon grew serious. Unused to genuine emotion as he was, it had always made him uncomfortable to attempt to speak from the heart. He never had any trouble knowing exactly how he felt, but never before tonight had he felt at liberty to express his feelings to anyone else. Communication was a door that could be opened and closed from either side; it was necessary for someone to be willing to receive before another could give. Jon was basically an honest and straightforward man who had been deprived most of his life of the ability to share truths and be honest about himself and others. No one spoke the truth in the theater, and no one wanted to hear it. But Stacey wanted to hear, Stacey understood. With her he was free to be nothing more and nothing less than himself. It was like a dazzling glimpse of daylight after years of imprisonment.

"I am too," he said quietly. His eyes were clear and steady. That was one thing Stacey had noticed about him right away. He had very alert, busy eyes that were constantly moving around the room in an almost nervous awareness. But when he spoke to her, or was listening to her, his eyes never moved from her face, as though what she had to say was of such import that it absorbed his entire concentration. That made her feel honored and special. "It was probably the smartest thing I've ever done. And"—the lift of his eyebrow was both amused and slightly self-deprecating—"I haven't done too many smart things lately. Being with you tonight has been"—his brow furrowed as he searched for the right words—"the best thing that's happened to me in a long time. I'm usually so keyed up after a performance that it takes me hours to wind down, and then I never do it completely. Sometimes I feel as though I'm living on nothing but nervous energy, waiting for the breakdown to come." His smile urged her to respond. "Tonight, just sitting here talking to you, I've been able to relax more completely than I think I ever have before. But it's more than that, you know." His expression grew serious again, though it was tinged with a slight uncertainty, as though trying somehow to convince her to believe him. "I feel comfortable with you. Close to you," he said simply. "I've never felt that way with anyone before."

With another person that statement might have precipitated a moment of awkwardness. At face value it sounded like a line. Jon was even, for a brief moment, half afraid she would be offended. But he should have known better. Stacey knew what he meant. He saw that even before she smiled and said, "I know. It's not too often that you meet someone you can really talk to."

"Maybe once in a lifetime."

"That's why I wanted to meet you," she admitted suddenly. The answer to his question, which had been so hard to put into words before, now seemed almost no longer to need explanation. It still sounded silly, and there was a touch of shyness to her tone, along with a slight coloring of her cheeks, but she was not really embarrassed to tell him anymore. It was a foregone conclusion that he would understand. "I had a feeling—from what little I already knew about you—that we would understand one another."

Jon loved the sound of her voice. It was soft and airy, melodious. It suited her appearance and her personality without a flaw, complementing and completing the whole woman. He could have listened to her voice, watched the changing expressions on her face and the movements of her delicate hands for hours. Jon could not help marveling over the rare thing that had happened to him tonight. He wished there were some way to tell her how much this had meant to him.

His eyes moved over the empty room, the scowling maitre d', and then, reluctantly, back to her. It was late. In some ways it seemed as though they had only been here for a few minutes. There was so much left to be said, so much more to be shared, that it seemed they had just begun. In another way it was impossible to believe they had only known each other for a matter of hours. It seemed like years.

He tried to make his expression rueful but there was no disguising the sadness, and the anxiety, that lurked in the back of his eye. "I think they want to close up," he said.

Stacey looked around the empty room. She felt both conspicuous and defensive. It couldn't be that late. Had they really been sitting here for over two hours? And the entire time it had seemed as though they were enclosed in a world of their own; the background noises and movements of the restaurant had faded into oblivion. She had easily forgotten that they were not the only two people in the world. "Yes," she agreed, hesitantly.

Jon knew he was being selfish. It was very late and she was probably tired. She didn't look tired. And in her face he thought he saw the same reluctance he was feeling. There was so much more. They had just begun to know each other. He did not want this special evening to end. He could not let her go just yet.

Stacey knew she would probably never see him again. That thought was almost too painful for contemplation. What had happened here between them tonight? Was it real, or only an extension of a daydream? She only knew that she wanted to hold onto it as long as she could.

I don't want to let you go, Jon thought.

I wish it could last forever, thought Stacey.

"We could go back to the lounge," he suggested, "and have another drink."

"Yes," she agreed immediately. "We really should let these people go home."

Jon smiled as he stood and paid the check, and

when Stacey turned to precede him out of the res-
taurant, he rested his hand on her back. It was an
unaffected, easy thing to do, and walking close be-
side her like that, he realized that the wildflower
scent that had floated around the conversation all
evening, so subtle it hardly registered as anything
more than the sweet atmosphere of her presence,
was her perfume. He could feel the delicacy of her
shoulder blades and the warmth of her body be-
neath the light suit jacket. Only now did he realize
how badly he had wanted to touch her all evening,
and it was better than he ever could have imag-
ined.

When they stopped at the bar to order drinks,
his arm was cradling Stacey's shoulders easily,
warm and strong and gently protective. The feel-
ings his closeness generated within her were both
heady and peaceful. Jon's touch, his nearness,
were electrifying, but it was only an extension of
the mental harmony which had been discovered
between them so artlessly. There was no way to
analyze the wonder that had come over her in the
last few hours, the incredible thing that had hap-
pened between them. It was almost too powerful
to think about.

The lounge was dark and nearly empty. There
was no music, and the two or three people who
lingered at the bar did not talk. Candles flickered
in red globes on the small tables, the occasional
clink of a glass or an ice cube was the only sound.
A late night laziness and intimate isolation were
the pervading atmosphere. There was a sense of
unreality about it all. Perhaps it was the combina-

tion of champagne and whiskey sours, the left-
over magic of the theater, the culture shock of a
dream fitting so neatly into the framework of real
life. Stacey did not try to understand it; if she un-
derstood it it might all begin to dissolve. Perhaps
she had wandered through the Looking Glass, but
it was a feeling she wanted to preserve. There was
a simple glow inside her, a subtle elation, a con-
tented wonder. She had waited for this moment
all her life without ever really having known what
it was. Maybe it was nothing more than a fantasy,
but to Stacey it was the most real thing she had
ever known.

She let Jon buy her a drink that she had no in-
tention of finishing, and they sought out a table in
a far corner of the room. As they were seated Jon
let his hand trail down her arm and close around
her fingers, holding her hand on top of the small
table. The clasp of his hand around hers was warm
and electric, and it immediately dispelled the
lingering daze of her senses, the dreamlike quality
that had surrounded the entire evening. Prickling
awareness tingled her skin like a low-dosage jolt of
adrenaline, awakening her to swift and clear aware-
ness of Jon and of her surroundings. It felt right to
hold his hand, but it felt strange, too. It was only a
satisfying extension of the camaraderie they had
already discovered, yet there was excitement in the
knowledge that the discovery had only begun.

Jon's face was shadowed and golden-tinged
from the artificially colored light, but to Stacey it
was starkly clear, close, and real. She could see the
smooth planes, the tight pores, the slightly coarse

texture. She could read his expression, gentle and introspective. The light in his eyes was a subtle, contented smile. "I have never," he said quietly and distinctly, "done anything like this before." His eyes were deep and serious, probingly sincere. "I live in a tight little circle that doesn't allow room for distractions. That's why I hide from publicity so much—I have enough phony props cluttering up my life without adding other people's opinions of me to the mess. It never occurred to me that there might be someone in the world *I* would like to know." And then he smiled a little. He held her hand warmly and easily, not stroking it or tightening his clasp, just holding it because it felt right to be touching her. "It probably sounds a little crazy to you because you have friends, relationships, people to talk to. I don't. I never even knew what it was like. But I knew I missed it. I'm glad I met you."

There was more. Jon wanted to tell her that he had never felt closer to anyone in his life. He wanted to tell her how rare and special she was, how complete she made him feel. He wanted her to know what a miraculous feeling it was to meet someone with whom he could share anything, to whom he could tell anything. But there was no need to say any of it, and that was the wonder that tightened in his stomach whenever he thought about it. He wanted to hold her.

"There are relationships," said Stacey thoughtfully, "and there are relationships. There aren't too many people you really have rapport with right away, do you know what I mean? I guess that's what makes it so special when you do find some-one.''

"Have you met many people like that, Sta-cey?'' he asked. It was not a leading question, an accusing one, or a flirtatious line. It was genuine.

She shook her head, smiling. ''No.'' And then, looking at him, she added, ''You know, I always thought, somehow, that you were a lonely person. I don't know what it was. Maybe it was something you communicated in your work, or maybe it was just the way you protected your privacy. It was as though you valued yourself and didn't share your-self with just anyone.''

The twinkle in his eye was teasing. ''Con-ceited?''

"No. Discriminating.''

Jon matched her mischievous smile, and it faded into musing consideration. ''Not lonely, though,'' he decided. ''Alone.'' Until now. How could he describe to her what it felt like suddenly to not be alone anymore? Loneliness was an isolated, self-imposed affliction, easily remedied with a few hours of shallow contact. But to be alone was something much more subtle, much harder to fill. Finding her tonight had erased the emptiness.

But Stacey knew about aloneness. She had never imagined that in the man she had admired so long from a distance she would find the other half of the whole—that she could feel, if only for this brief time, complete and filled. All she could hope for was not to wake up too soon, for surely this feeling couldn't last.

For Jon there was no question of it lasting. A bond had been established here that he had no intention of breaking. He wanted to explore its depth, to try its strength, to savor every bit of it. He wanted to be close to her and closer to her, to share everything each of them had to give. This was only a beginning.

Stacey found it impossible to comprehend that tomorrow might come and they would be little more than two strangers who had met in a bar. No, that could never happen. They had discovered something unexpectedly precious here tonight and it couldn't just disappear. There was so much more to be explored and shared together, and time had little meaning. She could have easily sat with him at this table all night and never grown tired of his conversation, never grown bored with his company. There was no other way to describe the warm web of companionship that had grown between them, except to say that it was comfortable. The comfortable feeling was knowing for a certainty that they could spend days or weeks or years on end together and never run out of things to say. It was knowing, somehow, that what was thought was understood before it was spoken. It was simply enjoying being together, wanting to be closer.

But they couldn't sit here all night. Stacey knew that. They wouldn't spend days or years together. And there was a desperate poignancy in that knowledge that she didn't want to face. She simply couldn't imagine herself saying good night to him.

"I don't want to say good night to you," Jon said. His smile was soft, sadly tender. He was afraid to look at his watch, but he knew it was close to two. He hoped Stacey did not realize how late it was.

She glanced around the room, a reflection of his regret in her eyes. He still held her hand, and it felt so natural now that Stacey could not remember when her hand had not been a part of his. "I think they want to close up here, too."

Jon said softly, "I want to make love to you." The words came out easily, without his having planned them or even having known what he intended to say, but the moment they were spoken, a peaceful sense of decision came upon him and he knew that was exactly what he wanted. To make love to her. With her. To hold her, to explore her and know her and share with her, to be close to her.

Beneath his hand her fingers stiffened, a brief spasmodic action that was instinctive in nature, but it nonetheless alarmed him. He saw her cheeks color, and her eyes shifted quickly to a point over his head, and even though he did not regret what he had said, she looked so vulnerable at that moment that he wanted to apologize. Yet Jon sensed—he knew—that she felt the same way he did. If she pretended to be shocked or embarrassed, if she got up and walked away without looking back, he would understand because he would know she did not mean it.

Stacey did not know why she was shocked. Surprised, perhaps. Caught off guard. The moment the words were spoken she knew it was what she wanted; it was only the unadorned deepening of the communication that had grown between them tonight, an extension of the warmth and rapport they felt for one another. She wanted to spend the night with him. She wanted to be wrapped in his arms and hold him and explore this precious fantasy to its very limits. She wanted to hold on to it forever. She did not want to leave him. They could not turn back and they could not stay here; the only choice was to go further.

Stacey looked at him, and he received the answer in her eyes with a smile. Not surprised, not joyful or relieved, just accepting. As though it was only natural. And then, once the decision was made, she could not take it back.

For just a moment, when she realized what she had committed herself to, Stacey's throat went dry and her heart started to speed. She avoided his eyes again, and her hand, which had felt so warm and comfortable nestled inside his only moments ago, was now hot and a little damp. She couldn't believe what she had just promised him with her eyes. Maybe he would think he had misread her. Maybe it wasn't too late to change her mind.

And then, just as easily as though he were finishing a conversation that had been briefly interrupted, Jon pushed away the awkwardness and guided them back into the unconstrained relationship that was second nature to them now. His smile was gentle and amused. "I'll bet you were scared to death when that guard came to get you."

Stacey laughed, though it was a little stiff. They

had all the time in the world; what was happening between them, what they were about to do, was only right. "Did it show?"

"Not a bit," he assured her. "You were the most composed looking person in the room. But I know how I would have felt."

Her mind danced back over the events of that incredible first meeting with a sort of detached awe, and she began to relax. It was so easy with him. "That man," she remembered, "the director?—he said something about your knee. Are you having problems?"

Jon shook his head, laughing softly. "George just likes to find things to worry about. He's assigned everyone in the troupe a specific injury or weakness, and we keep him happy by not telling him we're in perfect health. He's a frustrated neurotic, and everything goes a lot smoother for us all if we don't frustrate him any more than absolutely necessary."

And so they talked, easily and desultorily, for perhaps another five or ten minutes. When Jon took out his wallet and laid some bills on the table, it was the most natural thing in the world to do, but Stacey's mouth went dry again. As they walked out of the lounge his hand rested lightly on her waist, and there was nothing unusual or alarming about that either, but Stacey's heart was tripping in her chest. There was nothing in Jon's words or manner to indicate that this was anything other than the end of a pleasant evening together.

But Stacey knew it was not an end, but a beginning. When they got off the elevator, they would not go to separate rooms. And she knew that what happened next would most probably change the rest of her life.

Chapter Five

They were the only two people in the elevator. Jon dropped his hand when they got on and he did not resume the contact, and perhaps it was that that seemed to shatter the atmosphere of intimacy and companionability between them, precipitating awkwardness. Perhaps it was merely the act of leaving the lounge, walking to the elevator, making a conscious decision to push one button instead of two, planning to go to bed together.

Go to bed together. It hit her with a sudden jolt, and the sinking feeling that gripped Stacey's stomach was from more than the motion of the elevator. She was actually going to walk into this man's hotel room and take off her clothes for him, let him touch her. She could not believe what she was doing. She did not know whether it was excitement or sheer nervousness that was spreading a clammy film of perspiration beneath her crisp-looking suit; it was probably a combination of both. Her heart was pounding so hard that it moved the neat green lapel of her suit, and she turned a little, unobstrusively, so he could not see. And he had not even touched her yet.

But he was standing close. So close. She could hear the soft whisper of his breathing above the hum of the elevator, and from the corner of her eye she could see the rise and fall of his muscular chest. Was it possible that she had sat across from him this entire evening, talking with him, laughing with him, knowing him, and had not once been aware of him as a man, a physically perfect, electrically stimulating, sexual being? Oh no, she had been aware of it, all right. But everything had been so easy between them that she had not let his virility make her uncomfortable. She had not thought about those sinewy arms and powerful thighs, the muscular shoulders and hard buttocks. She had not thought about the strong, graceful hands and how it would feel to be touched by them. Now she thought about it, and it made her weak, hot with embarrassment, and quivering with uncertainty.

Stacey was not a woman of vast sexual experience. She had never done anything like this in her life. One did not just calmly decide to go to bed with a man, walk out of a hotel lounge and into a bedroom with him and proceed to make love. He had not even kissed her. He had not even touched her intimately or indicated that he wanted to. Yet—yet what they had shared was more moving than a kiss, more intimate than a touch. And that was why she did not at the last minute change her mind and get off the elevator at her own floor. She still wanted to be with him. She wanted to share with him and explore with him, to keep nothing in reserve. This was only the next step in what they had begun together, and it was right. It just felt rather awkward.

Jon did not speak as he gestured the way down the corridor toward his room, fumbling for his key. Stacey's mind was racing so, she hardly noticed. Her stomach was tight; she resisted the impulse to smooth her damp palms on her suit jacket. She could not remember whether or not she had shaved her legs before leaving for the theater. What would Josie think when she didn't return to her room until the early hours of the morning? That was a horrifying thought. Was this the way rendezvous were made? Where was the romance, the breathless excitement? She was excited, it was true, but it felt more like fear. The brightly lighted, pumpkin-color hallway was a drastic contrast to the dreamlike quality of the lounge, casting the two of them into a harsh and uncompromising light of reality. This was no fantasy; it was real.

If only he would touch her she might not feel so uncomfortable. But she was glad when he only opened the door, smiled at her a little, and stepped back, gesturing her inside.

Jon's room was a smaller version of the one she shared with Josie. Colonial reproduction furniture, pumpkin carpet, draperies patterned with a hunting scene. His suitcase was open on the tan ribbed bedspread, not yet unpacked, and he went to it quickly, apologizing, "We only checked in a couple of hours before we had to be at the theater.

I hardly ever unpack on the road, anyway." He closed the suitcase and lifted it from the bed, aware that he was rambling. Then he realized that drawing attention to the bed—freeing it for their occupancy, so to speak—might have embarrassed her. Jon quickly put the suitcase in the closet to give himself something to do.

When he returned Stacey was standing in the center of the room, looking more than a little uneasy. Jon swallowed on a suddenly dry throat, wishing more intensely than ever before that he allowed himself to drink something stronger than mineral water. He even considered breaking his regimen this one night and calling room service, but she would surely take that as a sign that he was as nervous as he felt, if she had not already guessed. It had seemed so easy down in the lounge, the natural thing to do. But, somehow, in the process of moving from the point of decision to the point of action, mundaneness had intruded. Before, he had wanted her in a warm, almost spiritual sense; now he wanted her sexually, and the combination of the two emotions was playing havoc with his nerves. He wanted so badly for everything to be perfect.

He said, desperate to break the oppressive silence, "The bathroom is over there, if you—" And he broke off, feeling idiotic, cursing himself. She knew where the bathroom was. Bathrooms were not what he wanted to talk about.

"No," Stacey said quickly, turning to put her purse on the table. "No thanks, I—" She was blushing. She felt hot and uncomfortable all

over. She wondered erratically what kind of un-
derwear she was wearing—not those silly days-
of-the-week bikinis with teddy bears on the rear
that she had bought at a bargain sale last month,
please. Perhaps it would be better if she did go
into the bathroom and undress privately, perhaps
she could wrap herself in a towel. Was that what
he wanted her to do? Oh, how *did* people man-
age this awkward business of going to bed with
virtual strangers? Someone should write a man-
ual. Someone probably had, only Stacey James,
simple soul that she was, had never read it.

He came toward her; he put his arms around
her. Though the motion was imbued with his nat-
ural grace and gentleness, it felt awkward, un-
certain. He drew her against him slowly, almost
hesitantly, and Stacey's heart increased its already
accelerated tempo at least twofold as he eased his
body into full contact with hers. Was there any
doubt that she wanted him? His strong thighs
were touching hers, his abdomen was hard and
firm against hers. The corded arms that glis-
tened with muscular power onstage were wrapped
around her, sheltering her, holding her as though
he were afraid she would break. A quick-creeping
flush spread over Stacey's body with the strange-
ness of being held by him, and every nerve end-
ing was alert and aware, waiting for his kiss,
wanting it desperately, hoping he would not be
disappointed in her.

But Jon did not kiss her. He simply held her.
Her arms slipped around his waist because she
was afraid he would take her uncertainty for a lack

of response, and she leaned her head rather stiffly on his shoulder. His hands remained firm and gentle on the small of her back, his breath soft and light against her ear. His heart was beating as rapidly as hers, and his face felt hot and damp against her cheek. The pace of his breathing was no more relaxed than her own. Stacey could feel firm, hard flesh beneath the silky material of his shirt, and her urge was to caress, to touch, to soothe. She kept her hands still, just as Jon did his.

Then he moved his hands to her shoulders; he stepped back a little to look down at her. He smiled. "I feel," he said huskily, "like a sixteen-year-old kid on prom night, all trussed up in a tux, with the keys to my dad's car in my pocket, waiting for the most popular girl in school to come down the stairs."

She sighed, letting relief course through her with the ease of his confession. "I haven't been this nervous since my first date in high school," she admitted, dropping her eyes. When she looked back up at him they were both smiling.

Jon slipped his arm around her waist. "Let's sit down," he said.

The only place in the room the two of them could sit together was on the bed; it would have been ridiculous to be nervous about that. The sudden break in the tension was like a gulp of cool air, which Stacey took gratefully, trying to relax. She sat on the edge of the bed in the curve of his arm, but he rested his weight on his palm behind her, not quite touching her. It was a companionable gesture, easy and comforting. She smiled at him. They understood one another again.

"Did you really go to proms, just like every other American boy?" Stacey wanted to know.

The tightening of Jon's lips was the beginning of a rueful grin. "Oh, yes. And some disasters they were, too. My parents were determined that I should have a normal childhood," he explained. "I sometimes think a normal childhood is the worst thing that can happen to a kid."

"I know what you mean," she agreed. "And if you think it's bad for a boy, you should have been a girl. All that anxiety—will he ask me, won't he ask me, and if he does do I say yes or no?"

He smiled, the twinkle in his eye playful and suggestive. "Are we talking about before the prom, or parked at Lookout Point afterward?"

Her blush was pretty and alluring, and the sparkle in her eyes matched his. "Both," she admitted. "Did you have a Lookout Point, too?"

"Every town with teenagers in America does. I think it's part of the charter." And then his smile turned tender, his eyes serious as he succumbed to the urge to tuck her hair behind her ear himself, revealing the small gold earring. It was an easy, affectionate caress. "Sex is very confusing, isn't it?"

Stacey met his eyes now, no longer uncomfortable. "It's been known to ruin many a good relationship," she said.

Jon touched her face lightly, letting his forefinger move across her earlobe, brushing the earring. His expression was sober and questioning. "Do you think it will ruin ours, Stacey?"

"I don't know, Jonathon," she answered quietly, for she couldn't be less than honest with him.

He had expected nothing else. He moved his hand over her hair, stroking it, loving the feel of its texture beneath his fingers. He watched her face openly, alert to signals of tension or alarm, reading every nuance that shadowed her smooth peach skin, her window-clear eyes. But she was just Stacey—the woman he had shared some of the most important hours of his life with only moments ago—receptive to him, open with him. Happiness and contentment began to build within him again, flooding the corners of doubt and nervousness with the daylight of her presence. Warmth spread over him, just from having her near, close to him again. They could talk to one another. "Have there been many men in your life, Stacey?" he asked gently.

Jon knew he had no right to ask that. He certainly had no right to feel as relieved as he did when she dropped her eyes briefly and gave a slight shake of her head. "My husband," she said. And she sighed, looking at him with a mixture of subtle amazement, confusion, and pity in her eyes for the children they had been. "We were so young," she said softly, musingly, sharing her secret thoughts with him. "We didn't have the first idea what life was all about. It's sad, to think of all we must have missed." After the divorce her friends had encouraged her to date, but the emotional paralysis which inevitably follows the death of a relationship had lingered until she was too busy trying to get her career started to give much thought to a social life. Since then there had been so many commitments, so many other things to dedicate her life to, that she had simply never developed an interest in a personal relationship—at least not the kind the men she knew could offer. She supposed it sounded deprived in this day and age to admit she had only had one lover, and that was seven years ago. Seven years. She had not, until this moment, thought of herself as growing old alone. Stacey wondered if her lack of experience would bother him, and that made her nervous again.

But Jon was looking at her very seriously, his hand cupped warmly over the satiny fall of hair at the back of her neck. He asked quietly, "Do you feel cheap?"

She looked at him, unable to lie. If cheap was not the word, it was very close—or perhaps it was merely her insecurity that caused this sense of uneasiness. It simply was not within Stacey's realm of experience to offer her body to a man on such short acquaintance and with so little consideration. The rules and values she had always applied to relationships had no meaning here, and she was not certain exactly how she felt. "A little," she confessed.

There was no condemnation in Jon's eyes, no hurt or sense of disappointment. His smile barely touched his lips yet she felt its tenderness. That gesture was more reassuring, more understanding, than any words could have been. He said simply, "Could I just hold you then? Just for a little while?"

She nodded, shyly, and turned into his arms.

Stacey felt the thumping of his heart against her ear, strong and steady now, and it was a comforting sound. It was wonderful to be held by him, to feel his solid strength and his tenderness, sharing with a physical gesture what their minds had been saying to one another all evening. Her hands felt the broad musculature of his back, the warmth, and the silky material; his hands spanned her length from neck to waist, cradling her in his arms. Their thighs pressed against each other's; her head lay upon his chest, his chin rested atop her hair, and they held each other, letting their bodies get used to the feeling of closeness. It was a warm and solid emotion, filled with all the rightness of the night.

Then Jon's lips moved against her hair, touched her forehead. She lifted her face to meet eyes that were deep and gentle, glowing with an inner contentment and a sincerity she had no reason to doubt. "You," he said softly, "are very, very special."

Stacey knew that. And so was he.

He touched her chin with his forefinger; she responded automatically, tilting her head. His lips brushed hers. The touch was amazingly soft, like velvet—a brief, tender gesture of affection. Then, hesitantly, he clasped her lips more firmly, testing, experimenting, urging no response. He lifted his face. His smile was sweet and easy, and it said for both of them what did not need to be put into words: There was pleasure in the moment; there was wonder in simply being together. Had she wanted it to end there, it would have. But neither of them wanted that.

Jon traced his forefinger lightly over the lips his own had so briefly touched. The feather-light touch was innocently erotic, quivering through Stacey with a promise of more. The shape and softness of her lips fascinated Jon. That was the first time he realized that she was not wearing lipstick, or if she had been it was gone now. The warm, luscious color, the sweet taste, were hers alone. That excited him, and he wanted to taste more, to explore more deeply. But his fingers moved over her face, intrigued by the texture and the shadings of color in her skin. It felt like satin to the touch, an artist's delicate blending of apple-blossom tones, flawless and beautiful.

The brush of his fingers was stimulating, opening her skin to awareness of him. The nervousness she felt now was more than an equal mixture of anticipation and anxiety mingled with uncertainty. Seven years of abstinence had restored her sense of emotional virginity, and this was like the first time; perhaps it was more important than the first time. Now she would be making love with a man, not a boy, and awareness of the nature of that man—Jon Callan, whom she had adored for so long in secret daydreams, with whom only this night she had discovered a miraculous and intensely personal relationship—stretched with a fluttering sensation from the pit of her stomach to the breathless cavity of her chest, making her ache with eagerness and anticipation.

Jon's fingers spread along the plane of her face; he lowered his lips to hers. His kiss this time was more than experimental, firm yet gentle, a kiss of deep affection that nonetheless hesitated before revealing more. That affection washed over Stacey in a powerful wave and was returned without thought, instinctively, genuinely, as her hands moved upward on his back and her lips parted in open response. That seemed to surprise Jon as much as it pleased him. Stacey felt his small catch of breath as the demand of his kiss deepened. His fingers threaded through her hair and tightened on her skull, yet gently, as though he were still restraining himself, allowing her to glimpse only the edge of his passion. Her lips were full and tingling, aching with the severance of the contact and the promise of more, when he released her, lightly kissing the corner of her mouth and the curve of her jaw. His breath was moist and unsteady on her heated face; now she could feel the increased rhythm of his heart, which was a heavy and powerful counterpoint to the tripping of her own. His hands moved to her shoulders, his fingers curling under the collar of her jacket. His eyes were bright and deep with an inner light as he whispered, "Will you take your jacket off?"

Stacey could not know how badly he had wanted all evening to see her body, shaped only by the softness of her white blouse, to touch her, and to explore the warmth of her through the silky material. It was both a question and a turning point; each of them knew that once the undressing process was begun it would not end. His mouth went dry when she lowered her eyes briefly, shyly, and she moved her hands to assist him in slipping the jacket off her shoulders.

Jon could see the tint of her skin through the full sleeves of the light garment; he could feel her warmth when his hands moved automatically to caress her arms. Stacey's heart leaped to a new and alerted pace when he lowered his mouth to the delicate ruffle at her throat, warm breath testing the pulse there. Her spine weakened with the sensation, making it difficult for her to maintain a sitting position beside him. A gradual shifting of his weight lowered her to the pillows, and a sweet, languorous warmth enveloped her, with the gentle nibbling and tasting motions of his lips on their upward path across her throat and her jaw. His tongue swept over her earlobe, tracing the semicircle of her ear, drawing a gasp of surprised pleasure from her when he drew the lobe into his mouth. She could feel Jon's smile of pleasure curve against her face, and he looked down at her, balancing his weight on his arms on either side of her, his hands cupping her head. His eyes were hazy and bright with contentment as he and Stacey shared the moment of discovery and promise. He dropped a kiss on her nose and then on the corner of her eye, and he looked at her again, his eyes deepening as he saw in her face the same quickening of response, the alertness, and the anticipation that were building within him. "Ah, Stacey," he said huskily, searching every inch of the open, eagerly receptive face beneath him. "I do want you."

He looked young, intense, vulnerable. Endearing and adoring. A little shy. His skin was flushed with a gauze of excitement and pleasure. She touched the textured flesh of his throat, testing the varying shades of heat and color, pressing her fingers against the dip in his throat and the winged collarbone, where the gold necklace he wore swung forward. Her fingers slid around his neck and she linked them together, her palms pressing into the warmth of his neck, silky strands of his hair tickling the backs of her hands. Stacey looked at him soberly, absorbing the wonder of him.

Jon lowered his face to her chest, pressing his lips to one pearly button. The fullness of her breast brushed his cheek and he turned his mouth to it. Honeyed fire rushed through Stacey as she felt the pressure of his lips, the heated breath of his open mouth. His hand cupped with delicate restraint and then with a growing urgency; she caught her breath as his teeth found and gently clasped her distended nipple through the layers of material.

He could feel the lacy wisp of her bra, abrasive and exciting against the damp silky material. He could feel the firm swell of flesh underneath. He tried to keep his hand steady as he impatiently worked the smooth buttons of the blouse, not wanting to tear the exquisite garment. Clumsily he pushed the material aside, undid the front clasp of the bra. His breathing was irregular and his eyes lightened and darkened at once as he looked at her, at the firm roundness of her breasts, almost too beautiful to touch. His hands cupped and gathered; with a groan he buried his face in her softness.

Every sense and nerve fiber within Stacey was honed to awareness of him, the heat of his face on her sensitized flesh, the firmness of his fingers. Her heart was shattering her chest, choking her. Quick, hot pleasure built to an aching anxiety, with the deep lingering kisses he pressed upon her breasts, the tightening of his fingers, the delicate licking and nibbling motions of his tongue and his teeth. She squeezed her eyes shut against the golden agony that was travelling on tight wires of desire from the concentrated attentions of his mouth to the core of her abdomen, spreading syrupy awareness lower where unsuspecting flesh pulsed in open response to him.

"Stacey," Jon whispered. His voice was rough and uneven. "Stacey."

He looked at her, his eyes alive with a subtle fire. His face was lightly sheened with perspiration, delicately flushed with desire. He caught the straps of her bra with the material of her blouse and gently slipped the garments off her shoulders, letting them fall to the floor.

The moment spiraled downwards into something intensely personal; no longer a fantasy, yet not quite real. Stacey gave herself over to it completely, letting her body guide her as well as her mind. Shakily her fingers found the buttons of his shirt and opened them, revealing taut, muscled flesh with each jerky downward movement. Suspended and waiting Jon watched the unsteady rise and fall of her chest, the intense, expectant pleasure in her face, the quivering of her parted lips with each breath. When she spread her hands over his bared chest and abdomen, he suppressed a moan of sheer, unexpected contentment; impatiently he shrugged out of the shirt and drew her to him carefully. The flesh-on-flesh contact was intoxicating. Her breasts swelled to an almost unbearable ache in response to the pressure of his smooth, bare chest; she felt completely surrounded by him, enveloped in his warmth and strength. Her fingers stroked the breadth of his shoulders, and his skin felt like silk. Drifting downward her hands discovered the ridges of his spine and muscle-sheathed rib cage, the supple flesh of his waist and the narrow band of material there. She tightened her arms around him, losing her breath in the cover of his mouth, unable to get close enough to him, to have enough of him.

Jon had never wanted a woman this intensely, with all his mind and his soul, and it frightened him. His urgency was hard to control but he did not want to rush it; he wanted everything to be perfect. A fever spread through him when he felt her nakedness against his chest; it shortened his breath and seemed to shake his whole body to the pounding tempo of his heart. He slipped his arm beneath her knees and gently moved her legs closer to him, so that she lay full length beside him on the bed. At some point she had dropped her shoes. Feather strokes of his fingers explored the length of one stockinged leg, moving over the small, delicate curve of her perfect knee, upward to where her skirt fell away to reveal a few inches of slim thigh, and further, stroking her hip, discovering the slender band of her bikini panties beneath the silken texture of sheer panty hose. As he shifted her weight toward him, his fingers tightened urgently on the curve of her buttock and he smothered a small groan in the perfumed warmth of her neck.

Stacey's hands moved restlessly along Jon's back as she arched herself into the firm pressure of his chest, wanting to melt into him. Her lips parted on a sound of intense pleasure and profound yearning as her unsteady fingers sought his chest, his taut, spare abdomen. His breathing was light and shallow, fanning rapid waves of warmth over her neck and her face. There was no awkwardness now, just the instinctive sharing of two people wanting to give as they received, selfishness and selflessness combining to form a perfect median. Stacey's tongue tasted salt and tangy soap on his shoulder as her lips clasped his flesh. She felt his shudder as her tongue swept over his breast, and that exhilarated her. His hand slipped beneath the band of her panty hose, and everything within her was frozen into alert response as his fingers spread over the softness of her abdomen, kneading and caressing, gently exploring. Then, in a sudden wave of passion too powerful to be contained, Jon gathered her to him again, giving her the urgency of his open mouth, his seeking tongue drawing from her, giving to her in the force of a kiss that seemed to last forever.

His leg curved over both of hers, drawing Stacey into the curve of his body, close, but not close enough. Jon felt the pressure of her nails in the small of his back, the unconscious yearning movement of her hips. Her hands moved upward along the course of his straining arms as he lifted himself to drop urgent, moist kisses all over her face, threading his fingers through her mussed hair, pausing just to touch her, to look at her.

Stacey's flushed face was drawn with the pain and the pleasure of desire, her lips were swollen and rouged from the frantic kisses they had given one another, her eyes were bright with joy and anxiety. All of Jon's soul strained toward her, wanting all of her.

His hand trembled as he took hers; her fingers curled shyly against his skin as he moved her hand over the oiled flesh of his chest and his abdomen. His light lashes dropped heavily with the pleasure of her touch, and she was unafraid, watching the softening and the intensifying of his face as he moved her hand lower and lower, guiding it to rest upon the powerful swell of his masculinity. A shuddering breath escaped him when he felt her touch there, the shy, yet encouraging, caresses of her fingers; all-encompassing, dizzying pleasure threatened to sweep him away. With great restraint, Jon placed only a single kiss upon the curve of her jaw; he let her hand fall away as he sat up and sought the fastening of her skirt. His fingers were thick and uncoordinated; the delicate closure of the garment frustrated him. He wanted to treasure every moment, to savor the slow revelation of her secrets to him, but the need was too urgent. At last the skirt and the filmy underclothes joined the scattering of other garments on the floor, and for a moment he paused, a look of wonder and hungry intensity darkening his eyes as they swept over her body. In another man that look would have frightened Stacey, but because it was Jon, the response that quivered through her was more like eagerness, anxiety, and need.

Jon stood, and in the full light of the lamps, he undressed before her. She caught her breath at the marvel of his nakedness, the perfection of every line and shadow, the flawlessness of this magnificent body that had thrilled thousands in the performance of his art, but was now hers alone. The patch of hair low on his abdomen was golden red, and the unashamed display of his state of arousal made her suddenly shy. She shifted her gaze until he lowered his lean, hard form beside her again.

Jon turned her face toward him; his smile was a blur of pleasure and desire as she felt the fullness of his unclothed body against hers. "Stacey," he whispered hoarsely. "Beautiful Stacey."

His hands stroked her body, soothing her, learning of her, and Stacey discovered the freedom and the lack of restraint that came with physical knowledge. She could touch him as he touched her, knowing for herself the hard muscles of his buttocks and his lightly haired thighs, feeling the breathless, urgent response she generated in him, as with each caress of his hands the burning need built within her to a nerve-shattering intensity.

His strong fingers kneaded her abdomen, pressing against the painful ache deep within her and promising to ease it, and Stacey went weightless, suspended in pinpointed attentiveness as Jon's fingers drifted lower, tangling in silky down, and lower still.

The sharp gasp she gave at his first gentle probings alarmed him; swiftly he pressed his lips against her cheek, tightening his arm around her shoulders, and he whispered, "Darling, I'm sorry, I didn't mean to hurt."

"No," she breathed, dizzied and raptured. "No." It simply felt so strange to experience a man's touch there, so strange and so wonderful, drawing her and guiding her into a new realm of hazy pleasure and concentrated awareness—a selfish alertness, a building agony that were both exquisite and desperate. Jon was breathing hard when he moved over her; through the blur of the promise he had built inside her Stacey saw his face—his raw emotions of need and anticipation, his eyes dark and intensely open. She saw the softening of that adored face as he guided himself gently into her; his heavy lashes drifted slowly closed with exquisite pleasure. And then her own eyes closed, her lips tightening on a cry of sheerest ecstasy, etching lines of magnificent yearning deep into her face.

He filled her. She had never known that feeling before. The quick, clumsy fumblings of her youthful marriage were no comparison to this; they were a distant memory of a shadowed past. He filled her, body and soul, he made her complete. She had never been aware of the emptiness before he erased it, she had never known she was searching until he showed her the answer. Where once there were two, now there was one, and she would never be whole again without him.

His movements inside her were slow and gentle, undulating, treasuring the sensation, exploring with delicate wonder the marvel of it. And she clung to him, savoring the sweetness of their union, spinning out the moment to its finest, shimmering threads. Stacey tasted the warmth of his lips, the drugging moisture of his tongue, heard his whispered breaths of tenderness and adoration. And the nature within them both drew them, pushing them onward, urging them with tantalizing promises toward the deepening of the journey. Their movements became more urgent, more demanding. Passion swept them into its own world, blotting out the present with a timeless plane of sensation and immortal drives. Blinding and mindless, the force that controlled them took them beyond themselves and into a place where nothing existed except themselves, showed them glimpses of immortality, promised them eternity. Stacey rose to meet Jon's mounting intensity with a ferocity of her own; smothered cries were lost in each other's mouths. She clung to him and he took her onward and onward, deeper into unexplored regions, higher and higher until the burning ache within her was stretched to its finest extension and snapped in a sudden, unexpected explosion, flooding her with wave after wave of dizzying, shuddering fulfillment.

Stacey was dazed, enraptured, in a world apart. Her limbs were tingling, and they felt so heavy and numb that they hardly seemed to belong to her. Dimly she was aware of Jon's kisses, slow and loving, on her face, but it felt so natural that it seemed it had always been so. She felt his weight like a warm blanket on top of her, his body still joined with hers. That was right and good. She wanted to stay like this with him forever.

But of course it couldn't be. Jon eased himself away from her, eliciting a small moan of protest from her until he drew her again into the warm circle of his embrace, sheltering her with his arms and legs. His breath fluttered in a warm stream across her face. She could feel the heavy pulse of his heart as it gradually sought its natural rhythm. Stacey hovered somewhere between the state of dreaming and waking, filled with a warm and heavy lethargy, wondering over the truth of what had just happened, far exceeding the depths of her imagination.

Jon was shaken, deeply moved, more profoundly touched than he had ever been before. He wished he could find some way to express it to her. He wished he were a poet, a master of words. There was nothing to be said that could approach what he had touched this night with Stacey. His fingers absently stroked a narrow path up and down the center of her abdomen where he had been, where even now a part of him lingered. He wondered over it, feeling almost reverent.

In silence they lay together, drifting backward from the heights of miracles to the warmth and security of reality. Stacey's body felt worn and wonderfully exhausted as her senses slowly returned to her again, but her mind was alert, renewed. She felt strangely as though she had been born afresh this night, changed completely, excited by the life that lay ahead of her, weary from the birth struggles. Jon said softly, "Stacey." His smile curved against her cheek. "Did we just ruin a good relationship?"

She turned her face to him, touching the shadow of his smile, feeling it reflected in her eyes. "What do you think?"

"I think"—his sigh and the rustling of the sheets were a whisper of contentment as he shifted his weight, drawing her even closer—"just when I thought it couldn't get any better, it did. There are no secrets when two people lie naked together, nothing to hide. I think this, right now, is what I've waited for all my life."

Her heart, which had only now settled into its slow, peaceful rhythm, pulsed suddenly and speeded at his words. That was just what she wanted to hear, what she felt. A foreverness that could not be changed. Forever, with him.

Jon's voice was a husky murmur, drifting away. His closed eyes cast shadowed crescents on his cheeks. "Stacey, I feel as if I could sleep forever. Do you mind if I turn off the light?"

"No," she whispered, her throat tight. In a moment he stirred and reached for the lamp, and darkness fell over them.

And lying with him in the darkness of a bed that was not her own, listening to the sound of his soft breathing, feeling his muscles go loose and relaxed against her, Stacey's mind began to race. A moment ago she had been lethargic and drowsy, now she was energized, as though her adrenaline level had just registered the incredible thing that had taken place in this room during the past hour. She couldn't help thinking. She had to.

Nothing could change this drastically in one evening. What had changed, what had happened? They had discovered one another, first on a mental level and now on a physical one. They had formed a spiritual bond that would linger within her forever, but what did it mean? Jon was still who he was, a man who had allowed her to touch only a corner of his life, and she...she was a woman who had just made love with the only man who had touched her in seven years. It was a profound experience, and rightly so. But nothing was changed. Not permanently.

They had both wanted this. They had discovered in each other someone to whom they felt an incredible closeness; they wanted to deepen that feeling. Stacey would not be ashamed of what she had done. It was an experience she would never forget, never regret. But she was still Stacey James, who had a long drive home tomorrow and a job to return to, a life filled with commitments and responsibilities. Tomorrow he would have no place with her.

And for Jon—she turned her head, looking at him, and she was swept by a wave of almost paralyzing tenderness and warmth at the sight of his sleeping form, his face so vulnerable and relaxed, so adored. Men never meant the things they said in bed. The most she could hope for was that he would not forget her, that he would think of her sometimes and know that once someone had loved him, completely and wholly, without reservation, for all of him. For she did love him. She had loved him without knowing him and she loved him more now, as though it were her destiny to do so. He could not be expected to understand that. But it was true.

She lay there in the shadows of the unfamiliar hotel room and a slow-creeping anxiety gnawed at the edges of her contentment, letting the diffuse and unwelcome rays of reality fall over her. She should not be here when he awoke. She did not want to expose them both to the harsh light of day, the awkwardness of confrontation as they tried to find their clothes and say graceful goodbyes. She wanted this night to remain forever sealed in time, a fairy tale with no beginning and no end, a memory untarnished to be taken out and treasured in old age.

She shouldn't be here. What would Josie say? Would she be worried by now? What would she think if Stacey came creeping in at dawn, disheveled? Stacey shrank from the image. Josie and she had been best friends for five years. They worked together; they played together; they had few secrets. Josie knew that Stacey did not do things like this. Stacey would be embarrassed to face the question and the surprise in her friend's eyes, and that awkwardness would taint the beauty of this night. She had to go back, now, while he slept, while Josie would not notice her entrance or register the time.

Jon turned over in his sleep, freeing her from his embrace. Stacey resisted an aching urge to kiss the curve of his bare shoulder, to leave him with a last good-bye caress. She folded back the covers carefully. She got silently out of bed.

"Stacey?" Jon turned over sleepily, his hand seeking hers in the dimness. It closed on her wrist just as she was preparing to step away. His smile was drowsy and shadowed, vague with sleep, but quietly aware. "It's very bad form to sneak away like a thief in the middle of the night, don't you know that?" he murmured huskily. "Besides, I thought that was the man's role."

She smiled affectionately at his half-asleep philosophizing, kneeling on the edge of the bed briefly to stroke his hair. "You can't sneak away," she whispered, "it's your room. Good night."

She started to get up, but his clasp on her wrist tightened. "Don't go," he said.

Stacey was surprised by the sincerity of the request. If he had ever been fully asleep he was no longer. She turned back to him, confused and uncertain. "Jonathon, I really should."

"Stacey, I can't sleep if you leave," he said simply. "Please stay. Let me hold you tonight. Let me sleep with you."

She wanted to. His face looked so young, so vulnerable. His eyes were so honest. A rush of tenderness flowed toward him and she could not refuse. She smiled at him, once again touching the satiny hair, which, even in the darkness, seemed to gleam and shimmer. "Permission to go to the bathroom?" she whispered teasingly.

"Two minutes," he murmured, and reluctantly released her wrist. His eyes caught a lazy light as he watched her cross the room.

She did not feel bashful about her nudity, for even under the cover of darkness she knew he watched her. This was the openness they had both sought, the intimacy that mere words could not establish. This was what it felt like to be close to one another. When she returned, he drew her immediately to him again, holding her with his arms and legs as though to prevent her escape. He need not have worried. She snuggled contentedly against him and that was where she wanted to stay.

"Stacey"—his fingers stroked her hair; his voice was quiet and serious and deeply reflective—"have you thought about it? Have you thought about what a strange and rare thing it was, our coming together like this? Somehow I almost knew that it would be like this from the first moment I saw you, that it would be this wonderful. That's a little frightening."

She touched his chin, loving him. Her eyes glowed with the contentment she felt. "How?" she insisted huskily. "How did you know?"

He looked at her very seriously, yet his voice was dreamy, faraway. "Because," he said simply, "you make me feel like I've lived before."

Her throat knotted with the depth of her emotion; she tried not to let him see how moved she was. "'When you were a tadpole and I was a fish ...'" she whispered.

"'And that was a million years ago in a time that no man knows,'"—he picked up the poem in a later stanza, his musing whisper a reflection of her own—"'Yet here tonight in the mellow light we sit at Delmonico's.'"

Caught in the spell, she picked it up in another passage, "'Our love is old, our lives are old, and death shall come amain.'"

"'Should it come today, what man may say we shall not live again?'"

Silence fell like a blessing on the echoing whisper of Jon's final words, and wonder enfolded her, overwhelmed her. The silent awe of a mating of minds was her glimpse of immortality. Her arms tightened slowly around him; she buried her face in his chest as her eyes stung with the unexpected blur of sheer happiness. "Oh, Jonathon," she whispered, "I love you so much!"

She felt his stiffening immediately as she realized what she had said; she knew it was the wrong thing. Panic stirred deep within her that the dream might be shattered so soon. Desperately she sought some way to back gracefully out. Jon turned his head alertly to look at her. Instinctively she knew she had to do something to ease the tension, to free him from the demand for commitment her confession must have seemed like to him. Words of love were not used lightly with Jon Callan. "I'm sorry," she said quickly. Her heart was pounding. "I didn't mean to—I just got carried away."

"Stacey, I—"

"It's all right." She stroked his chest; she tried

to relax against him, soothing him. "Let's go to sleep."

He was still, and after a while Stacey closed her eyes, trying not to think about the disaster she had almost caused. She wanted only to lie with him, to be held by him. For now it was enough.

But Jon did not sleep for a long, long time.

Chapter Six

Morning came, just as they both had known it would. Jon lay next to Stacey, his arm crooked over her head and his fingers brushing her shoulder, deep in his own thoughts as he watched her come awake.

He had to be on the road by noon at the latest. He had been awake since six, tensely listening for the knock on the door that he prayed would never come, some early riser asking if he wanted to have breakfast or run in the park. Neither he nor Stacey needed that this morning. They had these last few moments together, and the time must be choreographed very carefully.

All things looked different in the light of day, and the magical intimacy of the night before was already fleeing into the shadows of the morning. Stacey would probably be shy when she woke up, embarrassed to find herself in his bed and to have him look at her naked. Jon knew Stacey well enough to predict those reactions, and already he had discreetly pulled the sheet over her breasts to spare her that awkwardness. But beyond that he had no idea how she would feel, what she would say or do.

Last night she had said she loved him. Love. A powerful, all-changing emotion. No one fell in love in just one night. What had happened had been incredible; it had shaken both of them, but what could it mean for today? Women never meant the things they said in bed. He should know that. He did not know what was going to happen now.

Stacey's eyes fluttered open; drowsily they focused on his face. Quickly, before the alarm of full consciousness could register, he leaned forward and kissed her on the forehead. "Good morning," he said, smiling.

"Oh." She blinked rapidly, looking mussed and childlike and innocent as she tried to wake up. "Is it very late?"

"Not very." Jon swept her bangs away from her eyes, wanting suddenly and powerfully to make love to her, to banish the doubts of the morning with the memories of the night. But he sat up. "Do you mind if I use the bathroom first?"

"No. No, go ahead." Panic was already beginning to flutter, and Stacey shifted her eyes as he got out of bed and pulled on his pants.

She was grateful for the thoughtfulness of the gesture, which spared her the awkwardness of getting out of bed nude and fumbling for her clothes. She was glad he wouldn't be lying there watching her while she went from naked and wanton to cool and composed, trying to think of a casual way to say good-bye.

The secrets of nighttime passion had allowed no room for awkwardness, but today . . . today it was all different. Today she was just another woman awakening naked in a stranger's bed. It was happening to hundreds of women, perhaps thousands, all over the country on this Sunday morning, but Stacey was not comfortable in the role.

This was one of those sophisticated relationships, she realized suddenly. And how did those sophisticated people manage the morning after? *Call me sometime?* No, no, entirely too demanding. *It was really lovely meeting you.* She felt a hysterical giggle rising at the incredibility of the situation she found herself in. Stacey James, who had thought she could handle anything, hadn't the faintest idea how to get gracefully out of a man's bed and say a polite thank you.

Stacey leaned over the side of the mattress and scooped up her clothes. Without getting up, she pulled on her panties. The script on the front corner said "Saturday." It was now Sunday.

Jon would probably be embarrassed when he came out. He probably did not know how to handle this any more than she did. And after that awful faux pas she had made last night, he was probably scared to death. How could she have told him she loved him? He did not want to hear that.

As she stood up to pull on her skirt she noticed a small pool of gold on the bed by her pillow. She picked it up curiously. It was Jon's gold chain, and a tinge of unexpected color touched her cheeks as she realized she must have torn it off last night in the blindness of passion. Quickly she took it over to the dresser and placed it by the mirror, where he would be sure to see it. It had the look of something he wore constantly and it must mean a lot to him. She wouldn't want him to think it was lost.

But for right now the best thing she could do for him was to dress quickly and leave, so he wouldn't have to worry about an uncomfortable scene.

She was fastening the last button on her blouse when Jon came out, having taken time only to accomplish the minimum morning toilet. Stacey turned quickly to tuck in her blouse, but in the mirror she could see him—bare chested, his hair brushed and gleaming, his cheeks freshly shaven—looking not at all sorry to see her. And he said, coming toward her casually, "Why do I have the feeling you're about to try your famous sneaking-away-like-a-thief act again?"

Stacey smiled a little nervously at him in the mirror. She looked awful. Her hair was flat and stringy, her complexion sallow, and there were mascara rings under her eyes. She quickly took out a brush from her purse and did the best she could with her hair, answering, "Josie will be crazy if she wakes up and finds I'm still not in. You shouldn't have let me sleep so long."

"Josie shouldn't be worried," Jon replied carefully, watching her. "She knows you were with me."

And naturally she would reach the logical conclusion. Faint color stained Stacey's cheeks, and though it was uncomfortable, at least she didn't look so washed out any more.

Jon sat on the end of the bed, watching her so soberly that at last Stacey had to turn to look at him. He said quietly, "Sex *is* confusing, isn't it?"

So, he was not going to evade the issue. He was not going to pretend they were just two strangers who had enjoyed a tumble in the sack together. She loved him for that. They could talk about anything. "Yes," she agreed softly, closing the clasp of her purse. "Very."

He watched her alertly, his eyes bright and clear, busily absorbing every detail and nuance of the atmosphere between them, reading between the lines, demanding that she keep nothing from him. The question he was about to ask made his heart beat faster; the muscles of his stomach tightened in anticipation of her answer. "So," he said simply, "what happens now?"

He was leaving it up to her. Was she grateful, or disappointed? What could she answer? What *could* happen? What did he expect her to say? "I don't know, Jonathon," she said simply. "I guess we just go on."

That was not what she had meant to say, and she knew immediately it was the wrong thing to say. A brief flash of incredulity came into Jon's eyes, which seemed quickly to kindle a spark of anger. "Just forget we met each other? Just go on as if nothing happened?"

"I don't know if I can do that," Stacey admitted, and, inside her, despair and confusion were churning. What did he want? What did he expect from her?

"I know I can't," he said swiftly. A frown

hovered over his eyes and he clasped his hands tightly between his spread knees. The clipped tone of his voice suggested impatience, and he held his face so stiffly that a muscle in his cheek that she had never noticed before was visible. "Didn't I tell you last night that I had never met anyone like you before? Didn't you understand how much it meant to me to—do you expect me just to give it up?"

There was anger in his words, and the accusatory displeasure he directed at her threatened to shatter the fragile grip she had on her emotions. "Then what do you want?" she cried. "What do you expect?"

He released an impatient breath, dragging his fingers through his hair, regretting taking out his frustration and confusion on her. "I don't know," he said tiredly, after a moment. There was apology in his face, and he did not take his eyes off her. "Look, I know I'm being unfair. Nothing can be settled this morning. I just don't want to leave it like quick sex neither of us will remember in a week." His expression softened. "It wasn't like that, Stacey, for either of us. Was it?"

The quiet tone was more a demand than a plea for reassurance, and a lump came into Stacey's throat that she tried to hide. "No," she whispered.

"I just don't want you to walk away, and I don't want to think I'll never see you again," he said simply. "I wish there were some way to hold on to last night."

The lump in her throat thickened; impatiently

she blinked away the stinging film from her eyes. She could not lose control now. Jon looked so dejected and vulnerable, anxiously waiting for her to do or say something that would reestablish the warmth they had shared last night. What did come next? Promises of love and commitment? The old-fashioned till-death-do-us-part kind? It was too soon for that. To rush into rash declarations would make a mockery of what they had shared—as she had discovered so poignantly last night. But, surely, there was something to be said in memoriam. "We won't forget each other, Jonathon," she managed, and even mustered a genuine, if rather weak, smile. "We'll always be friends."

Jon looked confused, as though not quite certain that that was enough. But what more could he ask? Things were very, very different in the light of day. "What," he inquired cautiously, "is your definition of friendship?"

He had put control in her hands, and there was nothing she could do but accept it. She turned to pull on her jacket, and the rush of affection she felt for him overwhelmed her own sorrow. He needed her now, just as she needed him. That they needed two different things from one another was of no consequence. It was within her power to meet his needs, even if he could not meet hers. When she looked back at him, straightening the collar of her jacket, her smile was warm and simple, not strained. "A friend," she told him, "is someone you can call at two in the morning to get you out of jail. A friend is someone who says 'My house is your home,' and means it. A friend—"

"Is someone you can talk to about anything," he said softly, and he stood. That was what he had needed from her, and instinctively she had known. He came over to her, smiling tenderly, and he lightly placed his hands on her shoulders. "Will you be my friend?"

She looked up at him, her eyes wide and clear. He wanted to kiss her so badly it hurt. "I can't help it," she said simply.

"If I call you from jail, you won't hang up on me?"

Her smile spread slowly into a dimple; she relaxed beneath his gentle touch. "I wouldn't dream of it."

"Your house is my home?"

The sparkle came back into her eyes. "Of course."

Jon leaned forward and kissed her forehead, a smile of pure happiness spreading over his face. "Don't you ever call me from jail," he warned gruffly. "Anywhere else, but not there. I don't want to have to worry about you getting into trouble when I'm not there."

She laughed, finding it easier than she had expected to relax into his mood. She turned to pick up her purse and saw his necklace lying there. "Oh," she said, holding it out to him. "Your chain. I'm afraid I must have—" She blushed. "It must have broken last night," she finished lamely.

Jon's eyes twinkled and he closed her fingers

around the necklace. "If you broke it, I think it's only fair that you keep it and repair it. That will give you an excuse to visit me in New York, when you come to return it."

Stacey started to say that she hardly ever went to New York, but then she remembered the annual Special Education Convention which was to be held there barely a month from now. Maybe . . . .

"And also"—he turned and took up a sheet of hotel stationery, scribbling something on it—"my address and phone number." He pressed the paper into her hand. "I'm not so easy to reach, sometimes, so don't lose this. If I'm on the road my service will tell you how to reach me, but I should be in town after the end of May."

That was kind of him. Or perhaps it was only polite. Wasn't it protocol for a gentleman to give a woman his phone number after he had slept with her, just in case something happened? Though Stacey knew pregnancy was hardly likely to result from their night together, it was still a nice gesture—just in case.

She wondered if that was why he had given it to her. A very basic part of her hoped he was not having such practical thoughts and that he would not worry about it, but for whatever reason, she was grateful for his thoughtfulness. He wasn't trying to sweep her out of his life like a piece of used tissue. And that was part of why she loved him.

Stacey busied herself with placing the necklace and the paper in her purse, not knowing what to say. Good-bye, she supposed. This was it.

Jon knew there was much more that needed to be said. Once again he was frustrated with his lack of mastery over words. Another man would have known just what to say, just how to say it. Jon did not even know what he wanted to say.

With a small uncertain smile, Stacey half turned toward the door. "Well," she began ineloquently, and couldn't finish.

Jon touched her shoulder lightly. "I'll call you," he assured her.

Stacey nodded, managing to keep up her smile. That was as good as anything for a farewell line, she supposed. She turned and he opened the door for her. He watched her all the way to the elevator, sparing her the sound of the door closing on her retreating footsteps. Yet, closed door or not, it was over. Good-byes were just as final, whether spoken or silent.

He wouldn't call her. She wouldn't ever use the numbers on the paper he had given her. Last night had been a dream come true—but it was still a dream.

Chapter Seven

It was eleven thirty at night three weeks later. It was still too early in the year to leave the windows open, but the air smelled so fresh and earthy that Stacey couldn't resist. She huddled in the patchwork quilt she and Mimi had put together over the winter and tried to concentrate on the quarterly reports she was supposed to be compiling for the state, but a touch of spring fever had struck her, and it was hard not to daydream.

She had not made up her mind about the convention in New York. The school did not endorse any of her expenses and, traditionally, she had only gone once every other year, usually with Josie. She knew Josie couldn't afford the trip this year and, if the truth were told, neither could Stacey. It was only a three-day workshop over a weekend, and always before she had managed to spread her classes among other teachers, so that wouldn't be a problem. Neither could she use her grandmother's failing health as an excuse, as much as she felt she should; Josie would be happy to look in on Mimi while she was gone, but Stacey would feel guilty for leaving her alone again so soon. There were displays Stacey wanted to see, several classes she should attend. She supposed her car could do without that new set of tires a while longer. She wouldn't be using it much over the summer anyway.

Stacey sighed restlessly and tossed aside the quilt. She decided to take a glass of milk up to Mimi. She could hear the television still on up in her room.

Stacey had come back to the house she had grown up in, and to the woman who had raised her, right after her divorce. Her grandmother, Mimi Hargrove, had been Stacey's salvation after the death of her parents when she was twelve. Her father had been driving while drunk, and Stacey, too soberly mature for her age, had seen their deaths as a blessing. Her mother's health had suffered drastically after years of living with an alcoholic; she had been a frail shadow of a woman at the end, and Stacey doubted that even her husband's death would have freed her mother for living again. Mimi had taken in a grave, solemn-eyed girl of twelve and turned her first into a laughing, tree-climbing child, then into a mature, well adjusted young woman—a miracle the greatest psychologists of the country could not have wrought. Stacey loved her grandmother. But then, Mimi was a very special person.

Mimi was seventy-two years old. She had been widowed four times, and her last marriage had been at the age of sixty. Each one of her husbands was the dearest and the best. She had been a Radio City Music Hall dancer for twelve years. Her first husband, Stacey's grandfather, had been a big-band leader. From Mimi, Stacey had learned to worship music. She had not yet acquired Mimi's distinctive, fervent, celebratory reverence of life. She doubted she ever would. Mimi was one of a kind.

Stacey had never intended to stay forever when she had returned, stunned and disillusioned, to the Victorian house, with its gingerbread lattice-work, at the end of Mayberry Street. But she had never regretted for a moment her decision. Mimi, independent and free-spirited as she was, had never hinted to anyone how bad her arthritis had gotten, or that it was now complicated by the insidious onset of diabetes. They needed each other. Stacey had stayed.

"I saw that!" Stacey declared, stepping inside the door just as her grandmother whisked a stack of colorful brochures under her pillow. "Plotting treason again, are you?"

Mimi's eyes twinkled tolerantly as she gathered up the long wave of her hair and pushed it over her shoulder. The luxuriant tresses still glinted gold in places through the silvery-gray. "Come here," she invited, companionably patting the place on the bed beside her as she used the remote control to switch off the late movie. She retrieved the top brochure from beneath her pillow. "Just look at this. They even have tennis, for goodness' sake."

Stacey set the glass of milk on the bedside table and sat beside her grandmother, snorting over the retirement home brochure she showed her. "Shady Days. Sounds like a cemetery."

"Well, they do offer a discount on plots adjoining the grounds," Mimi admitted, deadpan. "When a person gets to be my age, she should take things like that into consideration, you know."

Stacey laughed and tossed the brochure back to her grandmother. "I'd like to meet the ad man who designed that incentive."

"Look," insisted Mimi, opening the brochure. "Spacious, artistically appointed quarters, each with separate patio and garden space. Nature trails, square dancing, two indoor pools, horseback riding—"

"Horseback riding! You're kidding." Stacey took the brochure from her. "I might just go there myself. Sounds like stiff competition for Club Med." She glanced briefly over the descriptions on the full-color page, not taking time to read the print. Mimi was not going anywhere. "When are you ever going to get this silly retirement home business out of your mind? You *have* a home. And you're a little too old to be thinking about running away."

"Precisely," agreed Mimi, accepting and refolding the brochure neatly for future reference. "After seventy-two years of faithful service it would seem to me a person has a right to look forward to her own retirement."

Stacey laughed. "You *are* retired, right here."

"In a place of her own choosing," added Mimi pointedly.

"Are you trying to say you're not happy here with me?" declared Stacey in mock horror.

Mimi's shrewd gray eyes twinkled blandly. "Well, my dear, I don't know how to tell you this, but it's not so easy for a person of your age and a person of my age to live together in harmony. That New Wave music of yours, for example, is just about to drive me crazy."

Stacey choked on a giggle. Mimi was the rock music fan.

"I miss the company of people my own age, Stacey," Mimi said, more serious now. "Is it too much to ask that a person be allowed to live with people of her own kind, with her own memories and experiences? Why, just like you. How good can it be for you to be cooped up in the house with an old woman all the time? You need to have more friends your own age and, perhaps in time"—her glance was sly—"even meet some nice young men. This is no kind of life for either of us."

Stacey sobered. This had been a running debate for the past year or so, and Mimi always confused her when she talked like that. Stacey was never certain how much of this retirement-home enthusiasm was generated from a real desire on Mimi's part and how much was born out of a sense of guilt that she was tying her granddaughter down. Stacey could not imagine that Mimi would really want to leave her home. And she could not convince her grandmother that she herself was here because she wanted to be, because of all the people in the world whose company she enjoyed, none could compete with Mimi. She decided to avoid the issue one more time. She did not like this kind of talk.

"Don't be ridiculous," Stacey said gruffly, picking up the glass of milk. "You wouldn't have any more in common with those old coots than I would. We're doing just fine, the way we are. Why are you always trying to foul up the program?"

"Those 'old coots,'" declared Mimi heatedly, "happen to be my peers. And they would never," she added derisively, taking the glass of milk Stacey pressed into her hand, "give a lady milk when what she really wants is a Château Lafite-Rothschild, 1969."

Stacey laughed, and just then the phone rang. "I'll get it in my room," she told her grandmother. "Drink your milk and stop giving me such a hard time, will you? If you don't watch it I just might move to Shady Days and leave you with this mausoleum all by yourself."

The telephone was on its fourth ring by the time Stacey reached her room, but she was in no hurry. No one called at this time of night except wrong numbers. She sat down at the little desk beside her bed and kicked off her shoes, lifting the receiver with an absent greeting. Nothing could have prepared her for the response Stacey was about to hear.

"A friend," said Jon Callan on the other end of the line, "is someone you can call long distance just to talk to. Did I wake you up?"

Stacey's heart leaped to her throat and back to its original position again rapidly, where it started pounding against her ribs in protest over the exercise. A tingling alertness spread over her cheeks and she lost her breath. "N-no," she stammered after a moment. "Jonathon!"

"So, you didn't forget me after all," he teased.

Even her fingers were tingling as though from an electric shock. She had never expected this. She could hardly believe it even now. Jonathon. "Where—where are you?"

"I don't know. Somewhere in Texas, I think. Is it very late back there?"

"No. Yes, I mean—don't you have a performance tonight?"

"I just finished."

"How was it?" She was speaking automatically, her brain not hearing what her mouth was saying. She was trying to absorb the fact that it was really his voice on the other end of the line. Why was he calling? What did he want?

"Lousy. I danced like an automaton. I don't want to talk about it. How are you?"

"You're never lousy," she corrected calmly. "You're just suffering from after-show letdown."

He took a breath. "I know. But pretty soon all the performances start looking the same to me, and I can't tell what's good and what's bad. I hate touring."

Now that her heart had stopped pounding in her ears, she could tell that he sounded keyed up, tense. She could almost see his restless fingers drumming on a tabletop, his busy eyes scanning the room, looking for everything and seeing nothing. A disturbed frown came into her eyes. "Why do you do it then?"

"Because I also love it. Don't mind me, Stacey. I'm just a little wound up—no big surprise. I stay that way. Sometimes I feel like a mechanized doll that someone sets on the edge of the stage every night, and then puts into a box until I'm needed again—only they forget to turn me off. I just needed someone to talk to."

"It sounds to me," said Stacey carefully, "as though you're feeling sorry for yourself."

"I'm entitled. I don't sleep, I don't eat, and I walk around twenty-four hours a day with enough butterflies in my stomach to fly the whole state of Texas right off the map." There was lightness in his tone, but now it dropped. She could see his tense fingers dragging themselves through his hair, hear his distracted sigh. "I don't know, Stace. Do you sometimes feel like just packing it all in?"

"A fifty-two week vacation on a deserted island? Palm trees and coconut milk and the waves lapping on the shore?"

"Tropical breezes and hula girls and rum punch twenty four hours a day. Don't they cook lots of fattening foods on tropical islands?"

"Not on deserted ones," she laughed. "Unless you want to roast a wild boar."

"My deserted island comes complete with a cordon bleu chef and all the accoutrements thereof," he informed her. Then he added thoughtfully, "I suppose the loneliness is the worst part. The isolation. Not having anyone to talk to."

"On the island?"

"Yeah." His voice was heavy. "I'm on an island

all by myself in the middle of the biggest city in one of the biggest states in the union. Or anywhere else for that matter. If that sounds self-pitying, it's supposed to. A little sympathy, please.''

"No one would believe this but me," Stacey told him, her voice soft with reprimand. "The famous Jon Callan, master of his art, the world at his feet, starving for attention."

"Which is exactly," he answered, "why I called you." There was a little hesitancy in his voice. "When do you think we could see each other again?"

Stacey looked at the chain she had hung over the frame of her mirror. She had had it repaired the first week she was home, thinking vaguely that she might mail it to him. The mail seemed so cold. "I might," she said carefully, "be coming to New York in a few weeks. For a convention."

"Is that right?" His voice sounded eager and pleased. The tension she had sensed there before was momentarily gone. "When?"

"The last weekend in May. I haven't made any definite plans yet."

"Will you call me?"

"Well, I haven't really made up my mind."

"What kind of convention?"

Stacey told him about the workshops, the special displays that would be set up that, through the manipulations of modern technology, would allow the teacher to experience firsthand the special problems of a handicapped child. He was fascinated, asking endless questions, offering speculations and absorbed observations. Through the conversation his tension began to evaporate, his voice relaxed. From there he told her about the cities he had visited after Boston, some sightseeing he had been able to do, some amusing incidents that had happened on the trip. He asked about her work, about Josie, anything to keep talking.

"I'm running up your phone bill," she had to object at last.

"I'm on an expense account."

"Have you had dinner yet?"

"No. I was too wired to think about eating. I guess I could have something sent up now, though."

She smiled warmly and secretly to herself. "So tell me something, Jonathon. Is it really all that bad? Do you really feel like packing it in?"

She could imagine his endearing, self-mocking grin. "Only before, during, and after a performance," he replied. "Otherwise, I'm just fine."

"Get some dinner," she advised him.

"I know it's late. You have to work tomorrow. Thanks for talking to me, Stace," Jon said sincerely.

"Any time."

Stacey hung up the phone with that same dazed, warmly intimate smile hovering about her lips. Her decision was made. She was going to New York.

She arrived on a Friday morning three weeks later and could no longer remember why she had been so determined to go. She got off the plane feeling

embarrassed, uncertain, and irritated with herself.
She had made the reservations impulsively, and
she had spent the last three weeks telling herself
that the enrichment of her education really was
worth the expense, that she owed it to her profes-
sion to keep current on new developments; and
she knew it was only pride that kept her from can-
celing the trip at the last minute.

To cancel would necessitate an admission to
herself of the real reason she wanted to go. Stacey
was not ready to do that.

Josie had been very discreet about the entire
matter since that morning Stacey had returned to
their hotel room flushed, disheveled and busily
nonchalant. Of course Josie knew what had hap-
pened, decided her friend's sex life was none of
her business, and made no comment. If she was
burning with curiosity she kept it to herself. But
on the matter of the trip Josie could not keep si-
lent.

She listened as Stacey casually unfolded her
plans, agreed it was advisable that at least one of
them should go, admitted that some of the work-
shops would be of particular value to Stacey's
field, and told her not to worry about a thing while
she was gone. Then, over coffee in the teachers'
lounge, she inquired easily, "So, have you heard
from Mr. Callan since we were in Boston?"

Stacey busily stirred her coffee, keeping her
manner offhand as she replied, "Once. He called
from Texas."

"Nice." Josie was noncommittal. "He lives in
New York, doesn't he?"

"Hmm."

"Did he ask you to come?"

Stacey felt like an insect pinned on a display board. Her cheeks were hot and she couldn't meet her friend's eyes. "Sure. That is, he seemed pleased when I told him I might come to New York, and asked me to call him." Stacey knew exactly what Josie was thinking. Of course he would seem pleased. Of course he would say, "Give me a call; we'll get together." That was only polite, for goodness' sake. What else could he say? But it wasn't like that, Stacey wanted to insist. He was glad she was coming.

"Did he, umm, ask you to come?" Josie wanted to know.

"Well, not exactly." And then Stacey knew what Josie was really thinking. There was pity and embarrassment in Josie's eyes, and Stacey's own eyes widened with hurt and quick denial. Josie thought Stacey was pursuing him, uninvited and unwelcome. That Stacey James had lost her head over a superstar, gone to bed with him, elicited promises from him he was unwilling to make, and was now hanging on to his coattails like some besotted groupie.

Josie's tone was quickly apologetic, "It's just that you hardly know him, Stacey. I mean, I think it's wonderful that the two of you, ah, got along so well and it *was* nice of him to call, I suppose, but I wouldn't get too wrapped up in—"

Stacey had said stiffly, "I'll see you later, Jo," and left the room.

But until this day the niggling suspicion that

Josie might be right, at least in part, had haunted her. And Jon did not call again.

You are chasing daydreams, Stacey told herself despitefully as she got off the plane that morning. You're making a fool of yourself over one incident, one mating scene that was no more important than the time it took to do it. So what if he called you from Texas? He was bored, restless. He just wanted someone to talk to. He *told* you that. It didn't mean that you had to go running off to New York to see him.

It wasn't as though Jon had actually asked her to come.

But she was here now, and she might as well make the best of it. Forget Jon Callan. That was not why she had come. She had a job to do.

Friday was crammed full of workshops and displays and Stacey had little time to feel sorry for herself, to be depressed, or to give much brooding thought to what the real purpose of her trip might or might not have been. She took copious notes and gained a sense of satisfaction from the amount of useful information she gained. It was far from a waste of time, and she would have plenty to share with Josie and the other teachers when she got back.

The learning disabilities displays were fascinating. She had read about them, but had never experienced them firsthand, and that in itself was worth the expense of the two-night stay. She was taken inside a booth where, with the use of mirrors and special lighting, her environment approximated the way the world looked to a child with minimal brain dysfunction. She was then asked to complete a simple test involving cubes and blocks, and she was surprised at how poorly she scored.

In another booth taped sound blared at her from four corners, each speaker carrying a different message. A voice chanted a nonsensical nursery rhyme, traffic noises screeched and faded, two people were having a conversation, and from one corner there was nothing but a series of irritating scratches and bleeps. In the midst of all this a smiling instructor tried to explain to her the directions for completing an uncomplicated logic problem, thus approximating the conditions under which many children with learning disabilities function.

In yet another booth she was asked to memorize and later write down three nonsense words that appeared on the screen before her. It was a timed test in which the words flashed on the screen for five-second intervals five times, allowing her ample opportunity to study them before she was required to reproduce them. The only trouble was that each time the words appeared the letters were in a different order, the characters written backwards or their positions rearranged. And when Stacey picked up the special pen to write her response, what she thought she wrote was not what appeared on the screen at all, and a punishing buzzer went off. She was astounded at how quickly her level of frustration rose—just like that of dyslexic children.

Jon would have been fascinated. As Stacey went through the displays she found herself absorbing details for him, remembering things to share with him, imagining what he would say about this or that, and sometimes even asking the questions he would have asked. She was enthused not only for her own sake but for the possibility of sharing it with him, and eagerness mounted to see him again, to talk to him, to watch the lightning changes of expression on his face, to see his eyes glow with interest and darken with thoughtfulness, to see the animation in his hands and expression when he talked. That was why she had come. Just to see him again. To enjoy his company, to relax in the easy relationship they shared.

By the time she got back to her hotel room, her head was spinning, and it was quite late. She ordered a sandwich from room service and showered and changed into her comfortable robe while she waited. She was postponing making that final irrevocable decision to call him.

Stacey tried not to think about it while she ate, because when she thought about actually picking up the phone and dialing Jon's number, her heart beat so fast that it was hard for her to swallow her food. And why shouldn't she call him? Just to say hello and tell him she was in town. They knew each other well enough for that. And, if he wasn't busy, if he sounded glad to hear from her, they could talk. She could tell him about the convention; he could tell her about the end of the tour. They always had things to say to each other. They talked so easily together.

She got up and slowly retrieved the sheet of sta-

Harlequin reaches
into the hearts and minds
of women across America
to bring you

Harlequin American Romance.

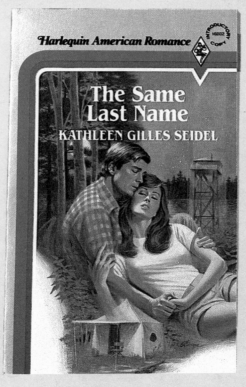

INTRODUCTORY COPY 16002

Harlequin American Romance

The Same Last Name

KATHLEEN GILLES SEIDEL

FREE BOOK...
AND·FREE TOTE BAG!

Get this Book and Tote Bag
FREE!

MAIL TO:
Harlequin Reader Service
2504 West Southern Avenue
Tempe, Arizona 85282

YES! I want to discover *Harlequin American Romance*.

Send me FREE and without obligation, "The Same Last Name" and my FREE tote bag. If you do not hear from me after I have examined my FREE book, please send me the 4 new *Harlequin American Romance* novels each month as soon as they come off the presses. I understand that I will be billed only $2.25 per book (total $9.00). There are no shipping or handling charges. There is no minimum number of books that I have to purchase. In fact, I may cancel this arrangement at any time. "The Same Last Name" and the tote bag are mine to keep as FREE gifts even if I do not buy any additional books.

154 CIA NAYG

Name	(Please Print)	

Address		Apt. No.

City	State/Prov.	Zip/Postal Code

Signature (If under 18, parent or guardian must sign.)

BUSINESS REPLY CARD

First Class   Permit No. 70   Tempe, AZ

POSTAGE WILL BE PAID BY ADDRESSEE

Harlequin Reader Service
2504 West Southern Avenue
Tempe, AZ 85282

NO POSTAGE
NECESSARY
IF MAILED
IN THE
UNITED STATES

tionery with his address and phone number on it. He wouldn't have given her his number if he didn't want her to call, would he? Of course she would call. He would be hurt if he ever found out she was in town and hadn't even bothered to phone. Of course he might not be home. He had said he would be in town by the end of May. But this was Friday night. Jon Callan had better things to do on Friday night than sit around the house watching television. There was only one way to find out.

Stacey actually had the receiver in her hand before she lost her courage and slammed it down again. It was already after ten. If he was home, he needed to be sleeping. She would call him tomorrow. Her heart stopped thumping once that decision was made, and she felt much better. Of course she must call him; he knew she was planning to be here this weekend and she was obligated to say hello. But she could do it tomorrow. Yes, tomorrow would be much better.

She stared at the phone a long time the next morning, and then, with sudden resolve, she knew she wouldn't call him at all. She wouldn't know what to say on the phone. She would go to his apartment. She still had his necklace to return, after all, and it would be much easier, much more comfortable, to see him in person. Then she would know right away whether or not he was glad to see her. Telephones were so impersonal. You couldn't read body language over the phone.

But midway on her trip downtown Stacey knew

she should have called first. One did not just show up at nine o'clock on a Saturday morning on someone's doorstep—someone one hardly knew.

But it was done now, and when the taxi pulled up in front of an unpretentious brownstone, Stacey knew it was too late to turn back. This was the best way, she assured herself, trying to calm the thumping of her heart as she entered the building and searched for the right apartment number. For one thing, if he was in town he would be sure to be at home now. It was early, but Jon had told her he was always up by seven, usually much earlier. Habit, he had said. Even when he had nothing to do, he couldn't sleep late. And she did need to return the necklace. She did not want to admit fully to herself that one reason she had decided on this impulsive visit was for the element of surprise. He would not have time to put on a false face when he saw her, even if he was so inclined. What she saw in his eyes—whether pleasure or annoyance, awkwardness or welcome— would be genuine.

With a deep breath she squared her shoulders and firmly pushed the buzzer. She could hear movement inside and she was relieved, but also swiftly nervous. He was home, he was awake, and he was about to open the door.

The door opened to the length of its chain and a woman's face appeared. "Yes?"

Foolishly Stacey checked the paper clutched in her hand again, stammering, "I—I beg your pardon, I must have the wrong apartment."

"Which number are you looking for, dear?"

Stacey told her, and the door closed briefly, only to swing open again once the chain was removed. "That's us," was the pleasant answer. "What can we do for you?"

The woman who stood before her was tall and classically beautiful. Her dark hair was loose and gleaming over her shoulders, her cheekbones high and prominent, and her lips curved into an automatic, though somewhat curious, smile. She was wearing a man's white shirt of sheerest gauze, and she was completely naked underneath. She was incredibly slender.

Stacey felt like a character in a soap opera, even as she idiotically tried to convince herself that she had the wrong apartment after all, that he had written down the wrong number or that she had misread it. And she stammered again stupidly, "I—I was looking for Jon—Jon Callan."

The woman called over her shoulder, but Jon was already coming into the room. He was wearing a brief kimono and nothing else. His expression at first was curious and not very welcoming, but when the woman stepped away from the door and he saw Stacey, nothing but quick surprise covered his features. "Stacey!" he exclaimed, and came to the door.

Had a hole suddenly opened up in the worn carpeting of the hallway, Stacey would have gladly crawled into it. If force of will had any power at all she would have disappeared right there before his eyes. Miserable color blotched her body from her forehead to her ankles, and she berated herself viciously, *You* idiot. *You set yourself up for this. How could you be so stupid?* She was not so much upset over the encounter as she was over the awkwardness of the situation in general. Innocent girl pays unexpected visit and the Other Woman opens the door. It was so trite. So cliché. And she had stumbled right into it, like Rebecca of Sunnybrook Farm visiting the big city.

Her embarrassment only increased as she saw the look of discomfort and awkwardness creep into Jon's face. "Stacey," he repeated, and tried to make his voice sound warm despite the fact that how he really felt was stunned. "I didn't expect—that is, it's nice to see you." And quickly, with almost a relieved enthusiasm at having at last found something intelligent to say, he added, "Won't you come in?"

"Yes, do," insisted the naked woman with an amused, almost wicked glance at Jon. "I was just about to make some coffee. Will you have some?"

Stacey stammered, "N-no, I—"

Jon said swiftly, "Stacey, this is Margie— Margie Lansing. Maybe you know her; she's my partner."

Margie gave Stacey a gay, vastly entertained smile and a wave, and then briefly ran her graceful hand over Jon's shoulder as she said, "My place is in the kitchen, love." Her eyes twinkled mischievously as she glanced briefly at Stacey and then back to Jon. "Give a yell if you need me."

Jon shot her a dark glance as she slipped away, and then turned distractedly back to Stacey. "Listen, it's great to see you," he began, talking rapidly, much too enthusiastically, doing his best to make the situation seem normal. "But we can't stand out in the hall. Come in."

He reached for her hand and Stacey backed away automatically. *Come on, Stace,* she scolded herself firmly, *you can do better than this. Let's not turn this thing into more of a situation drama than we have to.* "No thanks, really," she interrupted quickly, and she even managed to smile. She could have won an Oscar for that smile, for the even, almost casual tone of her voice. "I just stopped by for a minute on my way downtown." *Uptown, Stupid. You were going uptown.* She fumbled in her purse. "To say hello, and to give you this." She pulled out the necklace. "I wasn't even sure you were in town."

He looked at the necklace she dropped into his hand as though he had never seen it before. And then, quickly recovering himself, like a robot who had only suffered a momentary short circuit, he began talking again, "Well, that's great, but you can't just stand out there. Come in, have some breakfast with us, or coffee, or something." Before she knew what was happening, he had caught her wrist and pulled her over the threshold, calling distractedly over his shoulder, "Margie, is there any coffee in there?" Grinning nervously he added, "She's the only one who drinks the stuff. We just got in a couple of days ago and haven't done much."

Afterward Stacey would remember nothing about his apartment except a blur of neutral colors and a sweet, musky odor, like a woman's perfume. But then her eyes fell upon a tangle of clothing on the floor, near the sofa. A pair of men's jeans, a woman's blouse. A pair of lacey French-cut bikini panties and satin slacks. Had *their* clothes looked that way on the floor of that hotel room in Boston, flung off in haste, obscenely scattered together wherever they happened to fall, tawdry and cheap?

Jon was following the direction of her gaze, and he actually moved toward the pile of clothing as though he could quickly sweep it out of sight and out of mind. And suddenly Stacey didn't care about being mature or calm anymore. She did not care about being sophisticated and in control, and she was not going to sit across the breakfast table with Jon and his lover making bright conversation. She gave in to an overwhelming wave of claustrophobia and she turned.

"I—I just wanted to return the necklace, really. I have—a million things to do today and I can't—" She was talking just to hear the sound of her own voice; politeness was an automatic reflex as she made her way instinctively toward the door. "It was nice seeing you again."

"Stacey, wait, I—"

But she couldn't wait. She didn't even remember whether she proceeded to leave at a normal pace or whether she ran like a frightened child. She heard him call her name again, but she didn't turn back. She did not even stop until the sounds of street traffic were blaring in her ears and the nightmare was over.

Chapter Eight

It was the last day of the school year—at least for the students—and the excitement was palpable from the moment Stacey got out of bed. "I swear," she told Mimi as she cleared away the breakfast tray they had shared, "I think somebody sprinkles something in the air on the last day of school—stardust or something. Or maybe they slip it into the water supply, and it causes a whole national disease. I can't think of any other reason why a woman my age would be as excited about the last day as I was when I was eight."

Mimi chuckled. "Inherent memory, like riding a bicycle."

"Conditioned response," sighed Stacey, gazing through the sunny open window of Mimi's bedroom. A bird alighted on the high branch at eye level, and the warm breeze ruffled the starched white curtains. Already Stacey was wishing it were next week, when she wouldn't have to get out of bed, when she could spend the day puttering in the garden or sitting in the porch swing with her feet propped up, lost in a romance novel. "Like

Pavlov's dogs. The moment the first green thing pops out of the ground, we all start salivating, and by the time June rolls around we're certifiably crazy."

Again Mimi laughed, and Stacey bent to kiss her, saying, "I've got to run, or Josie will be here before I get my shoes on. Too much daydreaming has been going on around here this morning. You stay in bed today," she warned darkly over her shoulder. "You know what Dr. Bride said, and if I have to come home and drag you out of that garden I'm going to—to—"

"What?" challenged Mimi mischievously as Stacey could not think of an appropriate and believable punishment.

"Ship you off on a two-week singles cruise to the Bahamas!" retorted Stacey and hurried down the stairs.

This morning was the first time in two weeks Stacey had felt alive, cheerful, and herself again, the first time since that humiliating fiasco in New York, which even now she did her best not to think about. She had fought a valiant battle against depression and bitterness those first few days, and she had done a pretty good job, too. It was only when she lay in bed at night that the scene replayed itself in her head over and over again, and she writhed in silent mortification and sinking misery. That was what she got for being aggressive and assertive. So much for Josie's philosophy. Never again would she open herself up to that kind of rejection.

It was not that she was angry with Jonathon,

nor did she even allow herself to be hurt. She was angry with herself for being so starry-eyed, so expectant, so gullible. What did she expect, anyway? That she was his first lover? That he had been keeping that perfect body chaste and pure until Stacey James wandered into his life? Had she really believed all those beautiful words he uttered about her being special, about magic—for goodness' sake, what else was a man supposed to say when he was trying to urge a shy and awkward near-virgin into his bed? *You know better than that, Stace. Grow up.*

No, she was not angry. Or hurt. She did not even have the right to be disappointed. Men like Jon Callan were way out of her league. She should have known better. And the sooner she forgot the entire regrettable incident—and Jon Callan—the better. She didn't need the aggravation.

She hurried to get her morning chores done, as anxious as any of her students to have this day out of the way. Of course, technically this was not the last day of school for her. The teachers would report in for the next three days to wind up their paperwork and close the school, and Stacey only had a six week break before she began preparation for next year's work. Her job with the county was completed for the year, but the actual teaching she did with the children at the private school would require a great deal of evaluation and planning before she could begin to organize next year's course of action.

Stacey filled the sink with water to do the breakfast dishes, even though she would have preferred to leave that chore for another time. She knew if she left them there Mimi would inevitably come down to the kitchen for something, feel compelled to "just wash up these few things," and that would be the beginning of an entire housecleaning binge. As she stood gazing out the window with her hands in the soapy water, trying not to dawdle, the quiet peace of the morning was disturbed by the raucous roar of a motorcycle engine. Stacey groaned, thinking the Andersons' grandchildren must have gotten out of school early for their yearly visit. Stacey had nothing against the teenagers personally, but they did tend to be a bit rowdy for such a sedate neighborhood. And now, apparently, they had motorcycles.

But, in fact, it was not two motorcycles, but one that eventually came into view on the shade-splotched street in front of her house. Stacey winced and closed her eyes briefly, thinking it certainly made enough noise for two. She opened her eyes again when the roar dropped to a well-tuned echoing sputter, and found to her surprise that the shiny red and black bike had pulled into her driveway and was idling contentedly there. The rider cut the engine and dismounted, and Stacey wiped her hands on a dishtowel, moving curiously toward the back door to see what he wanted.

And there she stopped. Her heart paused with alarming certainty as the approaching figure pulled off his bright red and black helmet to reveal beneath it another gleaming helmet of distinctively unmistakable copper-colored hair. He ran his fingers through it, giving it a little toss in the freedom of the morning air; then he saw Stacey at the screen door and lifted his hand to her.

Jon moved up the steps with an easy, bouncy grace, smiling as he called to her, "Good morning." His smile was friendly and unaffected. "I'm glad I caught you at home; I was afraid I wouldn't."

Stacey couldn't speak. Even if she could have made her voice work she wouldn't have known what to say. She just stared at him, listening to the sluggish pulse of her heart and trying to remind herself to breathe, wondering if she could be imagining this. The dark mesh of the screen was scant protection from the power of his figure on the other side—tall and straight and beautifully shaped into skintight, faded jeans and a dusty black leather jacket, sturdy riding boots, and leather gloves, which he was just now stripping off and stuffing inside his helmet. His hair was oily and compressed from its long confinement inside the helmet, and there was just the slightest hint of a golden stubble on a face that was rouged with exercise and sun. His vibrant blue eyes were even more startlingly bright, reflected as they were by the pale strip of skin across his forehead and the bridge of his nose where his visor had come. There was no doubt about it. He was real. And here. On her doorstep.

The casual smile he had given her on first greeting began to fade into something slightly more serious, perhaps even a little self-mocking, as she only stood there, not speaking, not moving to invite him in. Though his tone was light, his voice was quiet as he reminded her, "Didn't you once tell me your house was my home?"

Stacey couldn't answer.

"I've come a long way to see you," Jon tried again, his tone softening. "I even"—the quirk of his brow was pointed and a bit wry—"took the chance that a man might answer your door. Couldn't we at least talk?"

Stacey's senses and coordination and voice returned in a rush and she moved quickly to unlatch the door. "Come in," she said. "I was just so surprised to see you. I didn't recognize you at first. Where did you get the motorcycle?"

Jon came into her kitchen, disguising his relief with easy strides and a quick, sweeping glance of his surroundings. Somehow he had pictured her in a place like this. Warm and old-fashioned, with a ceramic rooster on the wall and a daisy tablecloth in the breakfast nook. All that was missing was a bowl of yellow jonquils on the table. There was a whole patch of them along the back of her house.

He set his helmet and gloves in the center of the table where the jonquils should go, and replied, "The bike? I've had it for about a year. It's an easy ride. Handles well on the highway."

She looked at him in sudden disbelief. "You didn't ride that thing all the way from New York?"

"Sure I did." He pulled out a chair and sat down, wincing a little as he stretched his legs out before him. "Well," he confessed with an abashed grin, "It wasn't all that easy. But I took my time, camped out along the way, and it was nice."

She continued to stare at him, slowly absorbing the fact that he was here in her kitchen, that he had ridden that monstrosity all the way from New York to see her. And she really couldn't go too much beyond noticing the way the tight denim shaped his anatomy, hugging his knees and his thigh muscles and.... She swallowed hard and turned away quickly, saying, "Would you like some coffee? I've got some on."

"No, thanks. I can't drink it. But," he ventured, watching her, "I could use some juice, if you have any. It was a dusty ride."

"Sure," she said. Her tone was over-bright as she moved toward the refrigerator. "Orange or grapefruit?"

"I'll splurge. Orange."

Stacey looked like sunshine today. Her sleeveless shirtwaist was bright yellow, her hair mellow and gleaming on her shoulders. The low-heeled white sandals she wore made her look very young, and Jon's eyes followed every graceful movement as she went from the refrigerator to the cabinet, stretching overhead for a glass, pouring the juice. She had such small, delicate arms. He did not remember noticing that before. He was ashamed of the relief he felt that a man had not opened her door. He had no right to feel that way.

Jon smiled at her as she handed him the cool tumbler of juice. He smelled of good leather and sweat. Stacey went quickly back to the sink, plunging her hands into the cooling water, not knowing what to do next. Not knowing what to say. What was she supposed to say when he showed up at her back door at seven thirty in the morning on a red and black motorcycle— *Hi, there. Last time I saw you you had a half naked woman in your arms. What brings you out this way? What's new?* Had he done this just to get back at her for surprising him in New York? Was he hoping a man would answer her door? That did not sound much like Jon's sense of humor.

The position of the sink did not allow her to turn her back on him, and though she busied herself with sponging off the dishes she could see him watching her carefully, assessingly. Such clear, open eyes. They had never known duplicity or deceit. He was relaxed, in control, as though he had made up his mind about something and had long since passed the point of being nervous about it. She wished he could impart some of his composure to her.

He finished his juice and leaned back in the chair, unzipping his jacket over a lightweight denim shirt. And then he simply continued to watch her, choosing his moment, while Stacey's nerves tightened to the screaming point.

"Guess what?" he said casually, never taking his eyes off her. "Margie and I have been sleeping together for almost two years."

That was coming straight to the point. He didn't believe in skirting the issue, not this man. Stacey almost choked, but she controlled herself. In a way it was almost a relief to have it out in the open, to know he wasn't going to try to pretend nothing had happened. In another way Stacey would have liked very much to pretend the entire episode had only been a bad dream. Her voice was tight but even, as she replied stiffly, "How lovely for you."

Jon's eyes remained steady, his expression alert and sensitive. She knew he was cataloging every movement she made, every breath she took, interpreting them and analyzing them as he presented her with the cold hard facts. It was like a test. "There's a lot of tension in the theater," he went on, and his tone was as frank and as matter-of-fact as though he were explaining to her the intricacies of a new choreographic routine. "A lot of it's sexual. We both need the release; we'd go crazy without it. So we comfort each other in bed when we have to, once or twice a week, sometimes more, sometimes less, and then we forget about it. She leads her life, I lead mine. That's all there is to it."

Stacey's throat was tight, and there was a sick feeling churning in her stomach. She said exactly what she felt. "That," she managed quite cooly, without looking at him, "is disgusting."

"Yes," Jon agreed mildly, stretching one arm out before him on the table to toy with his glass. His expression was unflinching and undisturbed. "I suppose casual sex is the real social disease that afflicts the country today. But when that's all you get, that's what you take."

"I see." Somehow Stacey managed to walk over to him and take the empty glass out of his hand. "It was good of you to be so frank about it." She plunged the glass into the dingy water.

"I knew you were upset; I thought it would be best to get it out in the open."

"Upset?" Her voice was brittle. She couldn't help that. "I wasn't upset. Your personal life has nothing to do with me."

That was the wrong thing to say. That was less than he expected of her; she was acting like a typical hysterically jealous female. Stacey knew he was disappointed in her but she couldn't help it, that was how she felt. She felt hurt and betrayed and used, not so much because of the fact that he was sleeping with another woman, but because of his casual attitude about it.

His silence gently condemned her for the lie; his quiet gaze waited for her to make the next move. He had been honest with her, she had returned flippancy wrapped in a cloak of defensive hostility. The glass sloshed noisily in the water; she rinsed it with short, vicious movements and slammed it down on the drainboard with enough force to shatter it.

"All right." She whirled on him, her wet hands pressing against the back of the counter. Her eyes flashed in answer to his silent accusation and her voice was a little shrill. "I'm sorry, okay? I was upset—I *am* upset. I guess I'm just not as sophisticated as you; I can't look at it quite so clinically. But you want to be honest—fine, I can take honesty. So go ahead, let's have it all. How many women do you have, Jonathon? Is twice a week enough for you? Don't you sometimes do it twice a day? And what about positions—you forgot to tell me about positions. Let's not leave out any details, shall we? I'm fascinated."

Jon endured her onslaught without a change in his expression; his eyes were blank. "The usual positions," he answered quietly.

"Oh, really!" Her voice echoed with an annoying note of hysteria on the quiet morning air. "I would have expected a little more imagination from a man with your physical prowess. How very interesting. Well, well." She turned away, busily draining the dishwater and wiping off the counter with long, sweeping movements. She could hardly believe that the high, false voice dripping venom was her own, but it was too late to stop now. "I guess that just about covers it, doesn't it? Was there anything else?"

"No," he answered. His voice was maddeningly even. "That covers it. Do you feel better now?"

Stacey turned on him, her eyes blazing quietly. "Do you?"

"A little," he admitted easily. "At least I got an honest reaction. I was afraid you were going to try to pretend nothing was wrong."

Oh, damn. She turned away quickly before he could see the sudden sting of angry tears in her eyes, and she threw the sponge in the sink. She couldn't even stay mad at him, not when he was so infuriatingly open with her, not when she understood him so well. She jerked up a towel and began to dry her hands clumsily. "Yes," she admitted through a voice that was thick, but not quite ready to break. "Something is wrong. I am upset. I'm upset because everything you've just said makes the night we spent together seem cheap and—" She had to catch her breath before it dissolved into a sob. Her tone was quieter now, exhausted from such a rash display of emotion. "I don't want to admit to myself that it was. I don't like feeling cheap. Okay?" She swallowed hard, calming herself. "Honest reaction. Satisfied?"

Jon got up and crossed the room to her noiselessly. "What I have had with Margie was cheap," he said simply. "Meaningless. What you and I shared that night was not. You know that. Come on, look at me." Because she was afraid he would touch her if she did not, she turned around. She kept her body stiff and her chin high. There was sadness in his eyes, but tenderness in his smile. "You can cry if you want to," he said softly. "I understand."

At that moment she really believed that he did. And the understanding she saw in his eyes was almost her undoing. She blinked once, swallowing again, and said, "I don't want to cry." Her voice was weak, but it contained more conviction than she felt. "I have to go to work and I don't have time for this."

Jon searched her face with troubled concern— sorrow, hope, anxiety, and a dozen other emotions flickering through his eyes. Stacey wished she knew what he saw or sought in her face to put him through such a rapid vacillation of the emotional spectrum. "We're not going to let it ruin our relationship," he said softly. The force behind his words denied his gentle tone. "If I had known sex was going to cause this much confusion I could almost wish it had never happened between us. But I can't.'' The tenor of his voice dropped even further, sealing them with its husky half-whispering quality into a world where nothing existed but the two of them and the message he was trying to communicate, the depth of sincerity in his eyes. ''Because I made love that night. I never knew what the words meant before. I can't regret that. Please don't regret it, Stacey,'' he requested simply.

And then Stacey knew. She knew how special it had been between them—not just for her, but between them. It was something they had shared—two human beings who had stumbled onto magic, and whether they wanted it or not, it had left them both in some way changed. He could not lie about that, any more than she could. But it was so confusing.

Jon half lifted his hand, as though to touch her hair, and the moment hovered on the verge of expansion into something deep and powerful. But the blast of a car horn outside the window brought Stacey abruptly back to reality.

She glanced distractedly at the clock over the stove. ''That's Josie,'' she said quickly. ''I have to go to work.''

''We need to talk about this some more,'' he reminded her just as she stepped away.

Her mind was racing and so was her heart, and she simply couldn't stop to sort things out. But neither could she leave them as they were. ''Yes, yes, I know.'' She could do no more than give him a confused, harried glance as she swept her purse and her books off the washing machine. "I—I just have to go now. Call me."

"Guess what else?" he asked easily, and his movement across the room was a graceful contrast to her hurried exit as he held the door open for her. "I'm moving in with you."

Stacey almost dropped her books. She stared at him, open-mouthed, while his still, complacent eyes observed every changing expression on her face. He was serious.

"Just for two weeks," he explained, "until we start rehearsals. Don't worry though, I'm a good houseguest."

He couldn't mean it. He did mean it. He had come all this way.... "I—you—you can't!" Stacey blurted. "You can't stay here. I mean, I don't live alone, and you can't—"

His eyes narrowed with swift, unexpected emotion. "You don't?" His voice still sounded calm, almost disinterested. "Who do you live with?"

"My—my grandmother. It's her house. You can't—"

She was too distracted to notice the relief that flowed through him like a sigh. "No problem. I'm sure we'll get along fine."

The horn blasted again and Stacey took a hesitant step out the door, then looked back again, torn. "Jonathon, stop teasing me, I don't have time for it now. You can't stay here. There are a couple of motels out on the highway—you can stay and use the phone if you like." The horn sounded again. "Look, I have to go. Call me tonight and let me know where you're staying; I'm not trying to be rude but I have to—"

Jon watched her run down the walk, with an amused, affectionate smile on his face. Then he turned and went inside.

Stacey passed the day in a mixture of elation and apprehension, excitement and despair. She repeatedly felt the urge to pinch herself to assure herself that Jon Callan really had showed up at her door this morning on a motorcycle, that he really had come all this way just to—just to what? Should she be happy that he had cared enough about her feelings to explain his relationship with Margie? That was only Jon's way—direct, open. It was part of why she loved him. But there was nothing reassuring at all in his explanation. It only reinforced what she had already known on a deep and secret level: As much as they were alike in so many ways, they were poles apart in their attitudes about one important thing—human relationships. It had been a mistake to allow passion to insinuate itself between them; Stacey simply was not the type of woman who could handle casual sex. Jon had said their night together was special to him; she believed him. What had happened before they went to his room had been very, very special for both of them. What had happened afterward had meant much more to Stacey than it had to Jon. And, as much as she hated herself for it, she knew she would never be completely sure Jon had not used her that night just as he used Margie. The magic had faded from the fantasy the moment she had gone to Jon's door and Margie had opened it, and Stacey couldn't help it—she felt hurt.

Of course Stacey had to tell Josie who owned the shiny red and black motorcycle in her driveway, and throughout that hectic day Josie kept giving her twinkling, congratulatory looks. Stacey knew that her friend could not wait until lunchtime to get all the details. Almost gratefully, Stacey shared the story of Jon Callan between bites of a soggy tuna fish sandwich, intermittent food fights, one near-choking episode, and two temper tantrums. She omitted only two details— the interval between 2:00 and 7:00 A.M. during the weekend in Boston—the generalities of which Josie had already guessed anyway—and Jon's unexpected guest in New York. The one was too fragile for exposure, the other too disturbing.

"Well," pronounced Josie thoughtfully, carefully considering this latest turn of events, "I'm no expert, of course, but it does appear to me as though you have something rather serious going on."

Stacey could not prevent a wan smile. "On my part, you mean?" And though she tried to keep her tone light, a note of pathos slipped through. "Little did I guess, huh, that an overdose of champagne and imagination would lead to losing my heart to a superstar?" Then she shrugged, pushing her coleslaw around on her plate. "You know what it is with me, Josie. He's just a cardboard hero, every woman's dream. I was star struck."

Josie lifted an eyebrow. "You're not anymore?"

Stacey thought about it. "I'm not sure. I've never had a dream come true before. It feels strange."

"To find that beneath the perfect body of the ideal man there beats only another human heart?" Josie melodramatized, making Stacey smile.

"Exactly," she returned. "I'm not quite sure how I feel about the flaws behind the perfect body of the ideal man yet."

"Oh, I think you are," suggested Josie with a secret smile, but she did not give Stacey a chance to question her meaning. "So," she insisted, "what about him? Do you really think he came all the way out here just to be polite? Or is it totally beyond your conception that the great man might have a few human feelings for you?"

Stacey widened her eyes, disguising her mirth. "You wouldn't be the type to jump to conclusions, would you? A meeting, a phone call, a couple of visits, and you already have us at the altar."

Josie shrugged. "If you're going to fantasize, go all the way. So you tell me—why did he come?"

Stacey would have loved to have fantasized over that. She would have loved to give Josie's romantic imagination its full rein. But there she drew the line. She knew the facts too well. "Jon is a lonely person," she explained carefully. "I know it sounds crazy, but it's true. He values my friendship, that's all."

"Is that so bad?" demanded Josie incredulously.

Stacey smiled. No, it wasn't. In fact it was rather wonderful. So many people fell in love without ever being friends first. Other people committed themselves to marriage and family life without ever sharing true companionship with their partners. What Stacey and Jon shared was very special. To be needed by Jon in any way was a wonder, more than she ever could have dreamed of. If friendship was all he wanted, then she could surely give him that. And she would just have to ignore the fact that she wanted more from him.

But as the day went from its impossible beginning to its absolutely frenetic ending Stacey was fighting back a growing knot of trepidation and despair. Perhaps she had already destroyed the fragile kernel of respect and communication upon which her relationship with Jon was built. He had come to her with openness and honesty, seeking only understanding, and she had not exactly given him that. He was so insecure about relationships; he had had absolutely no experience with them. She had offered him the boundaries of their relationship that morning in Boston when he had asked her for a definition—yet, already she had broken her word. Was this the way one friend treated another? By ordering him out of her home after he had ridden three hundred miles to see her? She wondered if he would even call her tonight.

Until the very moment Josie pulled up in front of her driveway Stacey even held out a small hope that Jon might have waited for her. The shiny touring bike was nowhere to be seen, and Stacey was irritated with the lump of disappointment that formed in her stomach. It was best. What would Mimi have thought if she had come down to find a strange man in her kitchen? As avant-garde and broad minded as her grandmother was, Mimi was still a grandmother, and Stacey doubted very much whether she would approve of her grand-daughter inviting an unknown man to move in.

"You're driving tomorrow," Josie reminded her as Stacey got out.

"Right." Stacey tried to keep her worry from showing in her smile. "Eight o'clock sharp."

"Make it eight thirty," returned Josie. "What can they do, fire us?"

Josie waved cheerfully as she drove away, and Stacey stood for a moment in the warm summer sun before going reluctantly into the house. She was not looking forward to a long evening of wondering whether or not Jon would call.

The first thing Stacey noticed was a bowl of butter-bright jonquils on the kitchen table. She smiled in pleasure even as she formed a scolding lecture for Mimi in her head, and then a long shadow fell over her.

"I believe it was Robert Frost," drawled Jon Callan behind her, "who said, 'Home is the place that when you go there, they have to take you in.'" And he smiled at her. "Is your house my home, or not?"

Her first reaction was a gasp of surprise and in-stant pleasure that lit up her face and registered with a quick light in Jon's eyes. He hadn't left. She hadn't spoiled it all. "I—I thought you were gone. I didn't see your motorcycle."

"I put it in the garage; I hope you don't mind. It was drawing quite a bit of attention from the high school kids who walk home this way."

Stacey nodded, imagining it would. One rarely ever saw such a turned-out piece of equipment in a neighborhood as conservative as this. That silly, almost girlish glow of happiness was still warming every inch of her body, and she felt suddenly shy because she knew he must be aware of it. She said, shifting her eyes away from him briefly, "I thought you were mad at me."

Jon smiled. He looked beautiful, standing there in the kitchen sun with his fingers hooked casually in his jeans pockets, smiling in that warm, easy way that lit up his whole face. He was wearing a body-hugging tan T-shirt, untucked, and his feet were bare. He looked as though he belonged here. "I am the most annoyingly even-tempered person I know," he confessed. "You have to try a lot harder than that to make me mad. So," he invited with not a flicker of change in expression or inflection, "are you going to kick me out, or do I get to stay awhile?"

He was really serious. Why did Stacey find that so hard to believe? It was perfectly within the parameters of Jon Callan's personality to take her at her word and assume that he was welcome in her house at any time, or to test her sincerity. She turned away to put her books down on the table, thinking rapidly. "Jonathon, I told you, it's not that I wouldn't, that is, my grandmother—"

"Oh, don't worry about that," Jon assured her easily. "She's crazy about me. As a matter of fact, we spent most of the day playing backgammon and fighting over a box of chocolates."

Stacey whirled, abruptly paling, her eyes going wide with horror. Chocolates—the box she had bought as a treat for herself and had carefully hidden from Mimi in the back of a cabinet. "Oh, Lord," she gasped weakly. "You didn't—"

"Don't be ridiculous, darling," interrupted an energetic voice from the hallway, and Mimi came into the room. "The man's not an idiot, he knows what 'insulin' written on a medicine bottle means—much to my disappointment." Her bright eyes twinkled as she shared a grin with Jon. "I still don't see what harm one little piece of candy would do every now and then. I'm surrounded by jailers."

Stacey could hardly register her relief at the close call, or voice an objection to that fact that Mimi was out of bed and dressed for staying up, in slim brown slacks and a colorful top, before Mimi was declaring, "You know what I'm in the mood for?" She rubbed her hands together in anticipation. "A good old-fashioned backyard barbecue. Inch-thick steaks about medium rare, some of my famous potato salad, and, Stacey, you put together some of that delicious poppy-seed bread."

"Now, Mimi, you know I'm no good at cooking outside," Stacey objected distractedly. "Besides, you're not supposed to be out of bed. You—"

"Nonsense," scoffed Mimi with a dismissing

wave. She did not even bother replying to Stacey's last statement. "I'm sure your young Jonny here is more than capable of managing the fire—it's a man's place to preside over a cookout; it's in their blood. Now, if you'll just—"

"Mimi," said Stacey, blushing as she glanced at Jon's amused face, "his name is not Jonny, it's Jonathon—Jon." She wondered if her grandmother was purposefully trying to be difficult, just to confuse her more. "And he's not mine." Her blush deepened. "What I mean is, you can't just—"

Mimi's eyes twinkled at Jon. "Well now, I don't think he minds if I call him Jonny, do you, dear?"

"Not if you don't mind if I call you Granny," Jon replied equitably.

Mimi grinned at him. "Darlin', you just keep looking at me with those sweet blue eyes and you can call me anything you want. Now, what about that fire? Think you can handle it?"

"Well, I've never done it before, but I'll be glad to give it a try," agreed Jon enthusiastically.

"Fine. You come along and help me find the charcoal."

Stacey watched them with a mixture of amazement and despair as they wandered off arm-in-arm, and then there was nothing left for her to do but go up to her room and change her clothes.

Jon tapped on her door just as she was pulling a sleeveless tank top over her jeans, and she whirled in alarm and surprise. She wasn't used to closing her bedroom door and, sure enough, it stood half-open. She wondered how long he had been watching her.

From the casual expression on his face he had only just arrived. "We did it," he announced, obviously pleased with himself. He seemed more relaxed than Stacey had ever seen him, and the look on his face suddenly reminded her of that which had lit up her students' eyes when the final bell rang this afternoon. She couldn't help smiling at him.

"Good for you." She turned to gather up her clothes as he came inside. "I can't believe you've never lighted a charcoal fire before."

"I've led a sheltered life." Jon's eyes were traveling with alert appreciation over the details of her bedroom—the sprigged curtains, the skirted dressing table—finally resting on her bed. "You have a water bed," he commented with surprise and approval. "So do I, at home. They're great, aren't they?"

That was a perfectly innocent comment; there was no reason for it to make her so nervous. Stacey bent to place her shoes on the floor of her closet as she replied, "Mimi bought it—she heard somewhere that it was good for her arthritis. But it turned out that it was too hard for her to get out of in the morning, so she gave it to me."

"It's hard to sleep on anything else after you've gotten used to a water bed," Jon said reflectively. "That's probably one reason I have so much trouble on the road."

Was it only all this talk of beds that was making her pulse increase so uncomfortably, or was it his presence here in her room, in her house, still unexplained and unsettled. Well, this could not go on. She had to know why he had come here, what he expected from her, what his plans were. She faced him directly, and she kept her voice casual and pleasant as she inquired, "You never did tell me what made you decide to come out this way."

Stacey's tension registered in his eyes, through his shrugging smile. "I needed to have a quiet nervous breakdown, and this seemed like as good a place as any."

She smoothed her hands on her jeans and held her position. "If you wanted to tell me about Margie," she began, and her voice was even, if somewhat hesitant, "a telephone call would have done just as well."

He watched the movement of her hands over her thighs, and he couldn't prevent the slight dryness of his throat that was an automatic reaction to the shape of her. He had never seen her in jeans before. Always before she had worn those pretty, feminine skirts and dresses. None of her softness was lost for the casual attire, but it puzzled and disturbed him to realize how little he really knew of her. He found himself counting the actual times they had met, to keep his mind off the way his body was threatening to react to the memory of the last time he had seen the shape of her thighs.

He went over to the window, removing his gaze from her, not wanting to make her any more uncomfortable than he already had. "It's nice up here," he said, pushing back the ruffled curtain to the balmy afternoon breeze. "You can hear the trees rustling and the birds singing." And then he turned, his expression soft, gentle, and completely honest. "I just wanted to spend some time with you," he said simply. "It was an impulsive and completely self-serving decision, and I'll understand if you want me to leave. But I hope you don't."

How could Stacey hold out against such unaffected honesty? Especially when she did understand why he had come; she understood the way he thought. Jon wanted escape with her, the same kind he had found after the performance in Boston, from the pressures and confusions of his hectic life. He needed her, and she was helpless to refuse him. How could she deny him something that cost her so little?

But there were still things that needed to be settled between them. She could offer him her companionship and the shelter of her home—those things she *wanted* to give him—but she could not bear the thought of being only another warm body to him, a receptacle for his sexual tension. She had made that mistake before, and even now she was unable to face the shame she felt for giving in to the allure of daydreams and imagining that they could reach for something more. Their relationship was divided into two distinct factions: the human one and the sexual one. With luck she might be able to forget the latter and maintain the very special quality of the former. He had to understand that. He could not be so unfeeling.

Stacey felt heat creep around her neck as she

tried to put her thoughts into awkward, cumbersome words. "Jonathon, I—"

"I put my things in the sun room," he answered her unspoken anxiety. He was observing and absorbing every detail of her uncertainty and discomfort, taking it into himself, feeling it with her. "It was Mimi's idea."

"Oh." She could not voice her gratitude and relief, but it swept over her face. "Yes, that will be fine. There's a sofa bed—it's very comfortable; we've only used it once or twice. And it's private, away from the rest of the house, so you won't be disturbed. I'll—I'll make it up for you."

"That's okay, I've already done it." Still he was watching her, carefully, assessingly, and his expression was easy as he added, "Mimi wanted to know why we weren't sleeping together."

That caught Stacey completely off guard and the flood of color that rushed to her face was unpreventable. She stared at him, shocked and chagrined and thrown into confusion. She did not know whether her embarrassment was the result of her grandmother's bluntness or anxiety over why Jon had repeated the question to her. She blurted, "You—you didn't tell her about us in Boston?"

"No," he admitted placidly. "That wasn't what she asked me."

"Then—" Stacey swallowed hard, facing him evenly, with her cheeks flaming and her hands pressed together tightly. Her voice was calm now. "What did you tell her?"

Jon looked at her, his expression unreadable.

What could he have said? That he had done a foolish and almost disastrous thing in reaching too fast for something he could not even define? That he had hurt someone about whom he cared deeply, and that person was so fragile, so precious, that it even now frightened him? That he simply didn't know?

He smiled, sweetly and boyishly, and the tension that had been threatening so oppressively around them dissolved as he touched her arm lightly to gesture her out of the room. "I told her," he replied, "that I wasn't as easy as I looked."

Stacey laughed, a purely instinctive reaction that bubbled with relief; she was glad to have him here and to feel the old, easy relationship seek its natural niche again. "Has she been up all day?" Stacey inquired as they went down the stairs.

"No, just since you got home. That's why I suggested backgammon, I figured, that way, she wouldn't have to keep me entertained. Damned if she didn't win five dollars off me, too," he added with a reflective shake of his head. "And me the regional champion of 1972."

Stacey's eyes twinkled. "Just, for goodness' sake, don't let her rook you into a game of pool. The woman's a shark. Did she tell you she used to be a Rockette?"

Jon's eyes lit up with enthusiasm as he shared with Stacey the conversation he and Mimi had had, revealing to her stories about her grandmother's early show business days that even Stacey had not heard before.

The backyard cookout-picnic was like a party, with laughter and conversation flowing back and forth, anecdotes and show business stories snapping between the two dancers with vivid alacrity. Stacey was enthralled as she shared parts of both Jon's and her grandmother's worlds to which she had never before been privy, and as the light faded into a grainy night fog she sometimes felt as though she was slipping out of a reality too good to be true. Jon, who did not eat red meat, declared the grilled breast of chicken to be very near ambrosia and told them that the closest he had ever come to the outdoor taste was when he had tried to operate a hibachi in his apartment. The apartment, he confessed, wasn't livable for three weeks, but the meal was delicious.

When it grew too dark to sit outside any longer, Mimi, who was a video game enthusiast, challenged Jon to an opportunity to win back his five dollars. With a twinkle in his eye, Jon agreed, not confessing that his own arsenal at home included every video game yet designed in the United States or Japan, and he took vengeful pleasure in wiping Mimi off the board in the first game. Their competitive appetites only barely whetted, they soon lost themselves in the maze of bleeps, dots, and floating dragons, and as Stacey went to clean up the dishes she was aware of an electric glow of happiness and contentment that she could not remember ever feeling before.

Stacey watched them play for a while, occasionally challenging the winner. They were like children, she realized, all three of them—simple, carefree, having fun. That was why she felt so good with Jon. When she was with him, she could carve a moment out of time, safely immune from the mundaneness of life, and she felt young again.

It grew late, and Stacey knew Mimi would sit up all night if this mood continued. And she would not respond to suggestions or direct orders. So Stacey took matters into her own hands, with an exaggerated yawn and a gentle hint. "Well, you two can sit up all night and keep the world safe from alien attack if you want to, but I have to work tomorrow, and it's past my bedtime."

Jon, immediately sensitive, declared as she stood, "What? You're leaving me unchaperoned with the femme fatale? Sorry, my mama raised me better than that."

He got to his feet, promising Mimi a rematch, and though Mimi was perfectly aware that the two of them had conspired against her, she took it in good humor. She did not, however, attempt to disguise the disapproval in her eyes, and Jon and Stacey called only a pleasant good night to one another and went to their separate bedrooms.

Stacey could not sleep immediately. Even after the house had settled down, residual excitement and the strangeness of the day kept her awake. She kept thinking about Jon downstairs in the sun room, in her own house. She kept reviewing the evening they had had together, smiling over little things he had said, wondering over how well he and Mimi had gotten along. Was he really planning to stay for two weeks? He would be bored long before then. She wondered if he was comfortable on the sofa bed. She should have asked if there was anything he needed. But that was silly. He had made himself perfectly at home; he probably knew more about the house by now than she did.

That made her smile again, with a secret and unexplained contentment, and she turned over, finally dozing about midnight. She still was not entirely sure what he had expected from this visit, or what it would mean to her, or how she felt about having him sleeping in the room just beneath her. But she was not going to worry about it. She would just take one day at a time.

Stacey had become a light sleeper since moving in with her grandmother, immediately attuned to any noise during the night that might indicate she was needed. But when she awoke abruptly an hour later, she knew the sound that had disturbed her was not coming from her grandmother's room. It was Jon. He was up.

She pulled on a robe and moved quietly down the stairs, careful not to disturb Mimi. As she had expected, the hallway light was on downstairs, and the front door was open. Jon was standing on the porch in his bathrobe, leaning against the rail, looking out over the quiet street.

He turned when he heard her. "I'm sorry," he apologized softly. "I didn't mean to disturb anyone."

Stacey fastened the top button of her light fleece robe and let the screen door close silently behind her. It was a pleasant night, warm and still. Only porch lights shone on the sleeping street, and they made abstract shadow-shows through the heavy leaves of oaks and maples. She came over to him, concerned. "Couldn't you sleep?"

He grinned apologetically and slid his fingers into the pockets of his robe. "Chronic condition. Besides, it was so nice out tonight, I just wanted some fresh air."

The robe was a light blue terry cloth, three-quarter length, and Stacey knew he was naked underneath. Whether it was that knowledge, or simply being with him in the shadowed intimacy of the front porch, speaking in hushed tones because they were the only two people awake in the entire neighborhood, that made her heart beat faster she did not know. She could see the hard outline of his body through the material, the muscular buttocks and strong thighs, his knees and his calves naked below the hem. The gold necklace he wore caught the light from the hallway and marked the beginning of a deep V of exposed chest that went almost to his abdomen. She took a breath. "Look, I've been thinking. If you'd be more comfortable in the water bed, we could switch rooms."

He shook his head. The problem was not where he slept, but whom he slept with, or more accurately, the lack of the same. The last time he could remember sleeping deeply and peacefully had been that short time in Stacey's arms in Boston, but he did not think this was the appropriate time to tell her that. Not when she stood before him looking slightly mussed and sleepy, wearing that sweetly alluring night garment that covered her from neck to ankle and was printed all over with a field of demure cornflowers. He wondered what kind of material the robe was made of, and whether it was as soft to the touch as it looked.

"No, the bed is fine," he assured her. "I was just restless."

She hesitated. "Can I get you anything?"

Under the cover of night she blushed, because that sounded more like an open invitation than she had intended. But he only grinned and replied, "How about a pizza and a beer?" Then he invited selfishly, "Would you like to sit with me for awhile?"

Stacey could not refuse. She nodded and went over to the swing. He sat beside her and they were silent for a time, moving their feet in unison to generate a soft swinging motion, enjoying the peace. Jon wondered how she would react if he took her hand. "How old is this house, anyway?" he asked after a time.

"About a hundred years old."

"That's nice," he murmured. "Nice to think something man-made could survive that long. Has it always been in your family?"

"Pretty much. My mother was born here."

He took her hand, holding it against his thigh. She did not object. They were silent. Jon was glad she could not sense the slow, heavy pounding of his heart. He felt as though he were on a precipice and that a fickle wind could at any moment buffet him in either direction, but he could not keep silent any longer. Her hand was so small and warm beneath his. He did not want her to hate him.

"Stacey, I want to tell you something," he began with a breath. He felt her stiffen. He tried to soothe her with a slight tightening of his fingers around her hand. It didn't work. "When we parted in Boston, things between us were, well, a mess. I don't think either one of us knew what to expect from the future, or each other. Maybe we didn't even know what we wanted."

But I did, Stacey thought with a quiet, low despair. I knew, only I was reaching for daydreams, trying to hold on to a fantasy. It just wasn't possible in real life. She said tightly, "Jonathon, you don't have to—"

But he wanted to. His fingers tightened again, slightly. "You said it yourself; we had to go on with our lives. Well, that was obvious, I guess. But beyond that, I didn't know what to think, or what you expected. I knew how vulnerable you were, Stace, and all that time on the road, I didn't do anything deliberately to hurt you. I wouldn't do that. But you didn't ask for any promises from me."

She looked at him. "And if I had?" Her voice was quiet.

There was no answer to that, not in truth. They both knew that. He looked down at her hand. "I just wanted you to know," he said soberly, "that I didn't forget you, or what we shared, for one moment. I don't ever want you to think that I didn't value that night." Value it, he thought dully, Yes, he valued it. It had thrown his world into confusion, turned his opinions and attitudes upside down, given him reason to hope when he did not even know what he was hoping for. It had come closer to changing his life than anything ever had before. "I just—more than anything I hoped you would never look back on the time you spent with me with shame or regret." And he sighed. "I guess I blew that."

The street was very quiet; the well-oiled chain of the swing made only a muffled scraping sound as they moved back and forth. Stacey could feel the hardness of his muscle against her curled fingers, the warmth of his hand. She thought about what he had said. Was it shame she felt when she looked back on that night? Regret? How could she regret something so beautiful, so special? The only thing she was ashamed of was her own gullibility in allowing herself to imagine, for even a moment, that the fantasy could become real. And she was sorry that Jon now obviously regretted it. But mostly when she looked back on that night now, what she felt was confusion.

"I think," she said at last, carefully, "that we're both more mature than that." She could not prevent the tension that crept into her muscles with the next question. "It might help," she added evenly, "if I knew what you expected from me now."

Jon wished he knew the answer to that question himself. She had said she loved him. He had lain awake that night and many nights since, wondering over that, wishing he could have told her the same thing. But he hardly knew her. How could he love her? The emotion was much more complicated, much more all-encompassing than the bond of friendship—an easy conversation, a physical act that somehow seemed to be charged with magic. Maybe even now he was wishing he could love her, and knowing it probably wasn't possible. Only more daydreams.

What did he expect of her? Jon released a breath of frustration and confusion directed at himself, and he said softly, "Nothing. I don't expect anything, okay?" Then he smiled. "Now if you should ask me what I want—"

"No," she said quickly, and made a small move to draw her hand away. "I won't push my luck."

He did not release her hand. "Selfishness," he said soberly, "is the first requirement for a dancer; vanity is the second. I know I had no right to come here and ask you to take me in, but I needed to be here, to be with you for a while. To escape for a little while. Do you understand?"

Stacey almost smiled. Yes, she understood about escaping. For years she had found her escape in watching a Jon Callan performance; that night in Boston had been the ultimate escape into fantasy. That he should seek the same sort of refuge in her mundane world now was almost too ironic to be believed—yet it was sad. Because it only proved more graphically than before that there was no chance for anything real between them. Each of them only sought in the other scraps of dreams to serve as a resting place between bouts with reality. Yes, she understood, too well.

She assured him, "I'm glad you came." And

she meant it. She received the grateful squeeze of his hand on hers, and she wanted to snuggle up against him, to hold him and be held by him in the stillness of the night and the understanding they both shared. But of course she didn't. In his world anything was possible; in hers there were limits.

After a time Jon said reluctantly, "You have to work tomorrow, don't you?"

Stacey nodded. "Only until the end of the week. Then I get a break."

He released her hand slowly, stroking her fingers as he did so. "You should get some sleep."

"I know." She straightened up, looking at him hesitantly. "What about you?"

"I'll go in in a little while." The flash of his smile was unaffected. "I'm on vacation, remember? I can sleep late."

"You won't," she reminded him.

"Probably not."

Jon stood as she did, and he looked at her so thoughtfully, so enigmatically, that Stacey thought for one heart-stopping moment that he would kiss her. She did not know what she would do if he did. She only knew that she wanted it almost as badly as she feared it, and that it would be very, very hard to remember the danger if he took her in his arms.

But he only reached up and unfastened the clasp of his necklace. "I always meant for you to have this," he said. The corners of his lips softened with a smile that seemed a little shy. "Will you wear it?"

She hesitated. She did not know why she was so reluctant. Perhaps because her yearning imagination wanted to read more into the gesture than was really there. She said haltingly, "It—I thought it must have some sort of sentimental value to you. Did someone give it to you?"

Now his smile relaxed, and not waiting for further encouragement, he stepped forward and fastened the necklace around her neck. His fingers were warm against her skin. "No," he said. "I bought it for myself in Germany. And whatever sentimental value it has"—he looked at her soberly, resting his hands lightly on her shoulders—"is recently acquired. I want you to have it."

She lowered her eyes, filled with a sweet romantic warmth that surely attached more significance to the gift than was meant, and she touched the necklace lightly. "Thank you," she said. She knew she would treasure it, a symbol of one perfect night, a solid reminder that sometimes, even if only for a short time, dreams could come true.

Stacey smiled at him, briefly and softly, and turned to go inside. Jon watched her, aware of a disquieting ache inside him that had no origin and no cure. He only wished he could have given her something more permanent, more real. . . .

Chapter Nine

Saturday was the first day of Stacey's vacation, and she spent it busily. Even Mimi at last declared that Stacey's energy was exhausting her, and she enlisted Jon as her escort for a leisurely walk around the block. Stacey did not quite approve of that exercise, but she did not say so. Everything had been going so well these past few days that she did not want to do anything to disturb the equilibrium.

Jon was, as he had promised, a very good houseguest. He did not do anything to make his presence burdensome and was in all ways very helpful and cooperative. During the days, he and Mimi entertained themselves and apparently had a wonderful time doing it, although Stacey could not see what pleasure Jon could get out of watching soap operas and digging holes for Mimi's prize petunias. In the afternoons, when Stacey came home, they discussed the developments in those soap operas in absorbing detail, arguing over possible outcomes and complications with all the sincerity of real-life participants, and sometimes

Stacey thought they did it only for her amusement. Her admiration for Jon's adaptability and patience grew, because she knew he must be bored to death. But he never hinted to his hostesses that he found life with them anything other than perfectly agreeable.

Jon kept his own schedule and demanded nothing of them. He got up to run every morning before Stacey was awake, and he returned promptly at breakfast time. Once when he invited Stacey to run with him, she almost accepted, for even though she was no athlete, she had always thought a morning jog around the block in the coolness and dew would get the day off to a pleasant start. She was prudent enough to inquire how far he ran, however, and he told her without blinking that it couldn't be much over ten miles. That, of course, immediately put an end to that idea. She calculated that he must get up around five o'clock to complete a run of that length, and she felt again in awe of him when she was reminded of his tremendous status in the world of dance and the physical prowess it took to achieve and maintain that position.

After Stacey went to work in the mornings, she learned from Mimi, Jon spent an hour or two doing warm-ups and exercises in his room. Stacey, who was accustomed to preparing her grandmother's lunch before she left for work, doubled the order for Jon each morning, but he never touched it. In the afternoons he and Mimi played their endless games and watched soap operas and piddled about in the garden. Stacey waited every night for the announcement from Jon that he was leaving the next morning. A man as energetic and restless as he, as accustomed as he was to a fast-paced life and action-filled days and nights, would surely go out of his mind after a few more days of this.

Jon went out of his way to be agreeable and un-obtrusive, but it was, nonetheless, a strain to have a stranger in the house. He did not complain when Stacey served him fried eggs instead of poached in the morning, but she was chagrined. He said nothing when he watched Stacey mix up a coffee cake to take to school, but she felt guilty. And when he sat down to a meal so filled with fats and cholesterol that the surgeon general would have banned it on the spot, he only commented with a twinkle in his eye that this was his idea of nirvana. And Stacey, naturally, over his politely adamant objections, felt obliged to immediately prepare a special meal for him more in keeping with his dietary requirements.

She could not pretend that having him in the house was easy. Jon liked to shower in the morning; so did Stacey. They went out of their way to allow each other the first use of the bathroom, with the result that, by the time all of the vaude-villian "Please, you go first," "No, you go first" was over, Stacey was usually late for work. Furthermore she enjoyed long, leisurely showers, and now she had to change to quick, brisk ones, so that there would be hot water left for him. Jon politely folded and rehung the bath towels to dry; Stacey preferred to toss them immediately in the laundry hamper, so she would not forget to wash them. She therefore had to remember every evening to gather up the towels he had used and put them in the hamper.

Jon did not leave the cap off the toothpaste, but Stacey had a bad habit of squeezing the tube from the middle. She knew that annoyed some people, so she now had to remember to go back and straighten out the little crimps and folds she had made in the toothpaste tube before Jon used it.

Stacey liked to read or watch television in the evenings; Jon liked to talk or play video games. Stacey started to yawn around ten o'clock; Jon never tired. Stacey liked to have dinner around five thirty; she knew Jon was used to eating later, so she adjusted her schedule accordingly. Jon liked to have the television or stereo on all the time for background noise; Stacey treasured the silence. Jon turned on the lamps to full glare when he was in a room; Stacey preferred soft lighting. The list could have gone on and on. It simply wasn't easy, having a him around.

And for the length of his visit so far, she had not even been home during the days. She could not help but be anxious when she thought about the coming week when they would be at home all day together. They would surely begin to get on one another's nerves. How would she keep him entertained? And worse, there would be times when they could not avoid being alone together. She knew she would not be able to keep at bay memories of what had happened the last time they were alone together. And such memories had no place in this, her normal, mundane, every-day world. There was bound to be tension and awkwardness.

That was probably why she had found so much to keep herself busy this first Saturday. Of course she had her normal chores, to which she applied extra diligence because of the presence of a guest in the house. But she particularly wanted to prepare a nice meal tonight. She hadn't had time to do much real cooking these past few days, and she thought wryly that she must have succumbed to the age-old instinct of womankind to impress a man with her domestic accomplishments. But as she opened the oven door to baste the lazily bubbling roast, she suddenly stopped, staring at it in despair—the heat from the oven searing her cheeks and the lid to the roasting pan held in her mittened hand.

"What's the matter?" inquired Jon from behind her.

Stacey almost dropped the lid. With his natural grace and silence in movement, Jon was always sneaking up on her, and that irritated her on a very basic level. "Oh," she said, determinedly soothing her jangled nerves, even though she was unable to completely keep the bleakness from her voice. "I just remembered—you can't eat red meat." And the twelve-dollar roast that she had prepared to such perfection would sit in the refrigerator for days, while she and Mimi turned it into sandwiches and casseroles and soup. It was almost criminal.

"What? Are you kidding?" Jon's voice was immediately enthusiastic. "That smells delicious."

Stacey thought of the blueberry muffins, the fluffy potatoes, the fragrant corn casserole. The only things Jon would be able to eat were the green beans and fruit salad. And he did not like green beans. She slammed the lid back on the pot with a clattering sound as she finished basting the roast, annoyed with herself. "You'd think I'd be able to remember a little thing like that," she berated herself. "I should have cooked the turkey."

Jon lowered himself casually to a chair at the kitchen table, restraining impatience with an effort. "Give me a break, will you, Stace? Roast beef is one of my favorite foods. I have erotic dreams about it. Just thinking about it makes me salivate. I've been looking forward to this meal for half of my adult life. Relax."

She met the playful sarcasm in his tone with a glare and she turned away. "I'll make you something else."

He released his annoyance in a long breath. It wasn't easy living with another person. He had always suspected as much. This, no doubt, was why relationships were so valued and hard to maintain—there was a secret to getting along in the everyday world once the magic had worn off. Stacey used all the hot water and mangled the toothpaste tube. She tossed wet towels into the laundry hamper and made everything smell moldy. She tortured him with garden salads and white meat, while she and Mimi consumed meals fit for a king. But worst of all, she was so darned accommodating. Jon had been living with her for three days, and he knew less of her now than he had learned in three hours in a restaurant in Boston. Stacey treated him like a stranger, and a stranger of whom she was more than a little in awe. Was this why so few commitments were made today? Because of the awkwardness, the uncomfortable process of getting used to one another's eccentricities, the constant need for compromise? Jon had never thought it would be easy. It was a very complicated business, a relationship.

He said, very calmly, "Don't make me anything else. I don't want anything else. I will be very upset if you attempt to serve me anything else. Will you please stop treating me as though I come from another planet?"

Stacey tested the boiling potatoes with a fork, swallowing back a sharp retort. She took up the pot and carefully drained the water into the sink, inquiring as casually as she could, "Where is Mimi?"

"I left her chatting with some neighbors down the street."

Stacey turned. This really could not be postponed any longer. "Jonathon," she said levelly, "I know Mimi enjoys having you here—she probably gets lonely during the day, and it's good for her to have company. But I'm worried that you're overdoing it."

His eyes were quick with interest. "I've been meaning to ask you about that. What's wrong with her, anyway?"

"Well, she's a diabetic."

"Controlled?"

"Well, yes, but her arthritis is very painful."

"She's never complained to me about it."

"Well, of course not." Stacey was having difficulty controlling her impatience. "But the point is, she is not well. She's a seventy-two year old woman who tries to act as though she's seventeen—"

"Mimi is intelligent and lucid," Jon interrupted blandly, no concern whatsoever in his eyes. "It seems to me that she's just as capable of taking care of herself as you and I are."

"You are hardly in the position to make that judgment," returned Stacey stiffly.

He only lifted an eyebrow.

"The point is," Stacey pursued, uncertain whether she wanted to apologize or defend her cause, "she is supposed to stay in bed."

"For an hour in the morning and an hour in the afternoon, isn't that what the doctor said?"

Stacey swallowed hard in a sudden flush. She felt as though she were under attack. "That doctor is too liberal," she mumbled. "He doesn't know the facts."

"And you do?" Jon had been absently picking the sliced apples out of the bowl of fruit salad ingredients on the table and eating them one by one; at her pointed gaze he dropped the slice he had just taken up back into the bowl. "Sorry," he murmured. He waited for an answer.

"Yes," Stacey defended herself staunchly. "I do. Mimi is very fragile and needs a lot of care. She doesn't know how to take care of herself."

"Bull," said Jon flatly. "She's got more going

for her than you and I put together. Do you know what I think?'' He continued adamantly without waiting for her answer, ''I think you're smothering the poor woman with affection to fill some kind of need in your own life. And she plays along with you because she doesn't want to hurt your feelings, but both of you know it's not the best thing for her. It's a wonder she hasn't turned into a hypochondriac with all the false labels you've pinned on her, and it's only proof of what a strong person she is that she hasn't let you make her into an invalid. Look at it, Stacey,'' he insisted, ignoring her heightened color and her darkening eyes. ''This was the perfect refuge for you when you came out of a bad marriage; an invalid grandmother was a built-in excuse for you to avoid taking up your own life again. You're hiding behind her, that's what you're doing, and I don't see anything healthy about it for either of you.''

Stacey stared at him, her nostrils flared and her lips compressed against furious words she would have liked to throw back at him. Her breathing was choppy, and there was a sick feeling in her stomach because this was the closest they had come to fighting since that morning he had told her about Margie. She would not lose her temper with him. She would not dignify his accusations with a reply. She did not want to fight with him. He had no right to say those things, but she would not be goaded. She turned away stiffly. ''I'm doing laundry this afternoon,'' she said cooly. ''If you have anything you want washed just put it in—''

The chair scraped as Jon got up and crossed the room to her in two easy strides. "I know how to operate a washing machine." His voice was clipped. "I can do my own laundry. Will you for heaven's sake stop treating me so much like a guest and a little bit more like a human being?" He caught her arm and turned her around. His eyes were dark, but his voice was even, almost casual. "Do you know what else I think? I think you're hiding behind me, too. I think that night in Boston you were doing nothing more than living out a fantasy with me—safe and secure because the nice thing about fantasies is that they never come true, and what isn't real can't hurt you, can it?"

A horrified gasp escaped her and she tried to pull her arm away, but his fingers tightened. There was an alien flicker of a blaze deep within his ice-blue eyes that she had never imagined could be there before. But still Jon kept his tone even. "Do you think I used you, Stacey? Is that the ugly little suspicion you've been nursing these past weeks? What about the way you used me?"

Stacey opened her mouth for an angry protest, but there was nothing she could say. He knew it and he continued intrepidly, "You've kept yourself safe and secure from involvements with men for seven years. A woman your age—for seven years"—he interrupted himself incredulously—"protecting yourself with words like obligation and responsibilities and being needed, and when you finally do decide to see to your needs for once, who do you pick? A man you don't know and will probably never see again, a fantasy figure you feel safe with, with whom you don't have to risk anything because he isn't real. It scared you to death the next morning when you thought I was going to ask something of you, didn't it?''

Her heart was pounding and her throat was dry. She felt pinned beneath the force of Jon's gaze and the arrow-sharp accuracy of his words, stripped and squirming, unable to defend herself. And Stacey was angry because he had hit so close to the truth, brutally knocking down the fragile walls that separated what she wanted to see from the harshness of the truths he was trying to force on her. And she gasped furiously, ''I—that's not fair! If I hadn't wanted to see you again, if I had wanted to end it that morning and just—just pretend it was a dream, I never would have come to New York.''

Jon looked at her, strangely and thoughtfully. ''You came to New York,'' he said slowly, ''hoping you would find exactly what you did. Trying to prove to yourself that nothing meaningful was possible between us. It was starting to look a little too good to you, wasn't it? A little too real. If it hadn't been a woman you would have found something else, anything to assure yourself what happened between us that one night was just a fluke, not real, so you could go home feeling hurt and disillusioned and telling yourself that I was out of your system and you would never trust another man again.'' His quiet gaze commanded, *Tell me. Tell me I'm wrong.* But she couldn't. She was too shocked to do anything but strike back.

"You're the one who couldn't handle the truth!" Stacey cried indignantly. "You were living two lives, hoping I would never intrude on your real world. Well, I did and you can't face the fact that nothing will ever be the same." She had to pause for breath. Tremors of emotional expenditure were threatening to communicate themselves to him, and she stiffened herself against them. Her cheeks were hot and her breath was coming rapidly, but she managed to cool her tone somewhat. "You admitted," she said tightly, "that you came here just to get away from it all. Don't sound so high and mighty when you accuse me of living out a fantasy—that's what you're doing right now!" Her voice was getting shrill again. "Only it's not working out quite the way you planned, is it?"

Jon looked at her intensely, his eyes widening and darkening as he considered the truth of what she said, and saw even more. His fingers, with their unconscious strength, were biting painfully into Stacey's arm but he was unaware of it. "Maybe so," he admitted carefully, tightly, "but not in the way you think. I thought I was the one who was ignorant about relationships, but you have an even bigger problem than I do. You don't want me here, do you?" he challenged. "You don't want to take a chance that we might find out we can actually get along together on an everyday basis, and you've done everything in your power to put distance between us since I got here. I've been living with you for three days, and I saw more of you in one night in Boston. It's as though

you're afraid I'll melt if I ever have to face
an overcooked meal or use a dirty towel or see
you without your makeup on. Damn it, Stacey,"
he said, frustrated, "that's all part of real life.
This"—he made a futile gesture around the room
to include the unwashed pans in the sink and the
fragrant roast in the oven—"and this." He pulled
her against him.

He had intended only to hold her, to feel their
bodies touching one another, to erase her cool-
ness with the reassurance of his warmth. But the
moment her thighs came against his, the moment
her breasts brushed his chest and the soft warmth
of her abdomen touched the muscled firmness of
his, Jon felt an uncontrollable surge of strength in
his loins. She felt it too and started to step back,
but his hands automatically covered her hips,
pressing her into him. High emotion, frustrated
communication, and pent-up desire erased the
control he had exercised so carefully these past
days, and he sought her mouth.

It was as much the unexpectedness of the mo-
tion as the wonder of his closeness that caught
Stacey's breath in her throat and made her heart
lurch against her chest. She put her hands on his
waist to steady herself and heat fanned through
her as she felt the urgency of his mouth on hers,
his body hardening against hers. Her arms trav-
eled around his back, fingers dragging against the
soft material of his T-shirt, feeling iron strength
beneath. Her knees sagged as he parted her lips
and the warmth of his tongue filled her.

Jon knew he should feel guilty, just as he knew

what he was demanding of her was wrong. But all his careful resolutions, the silent promises he had made to himself and to Stacey never to give her cause to accuse him of using her or cheapening her again melted into the need for her. He needed her as more than just a memory. He wanted her now as he had wanted her then, all of her, close to him. He was frustrated with barriers and thin illusions. He wanted to hold her, to know her, to be a part of her again. He wanted to slip his hand beneath the waistband of her jeans and feel her flesh on his palm. He wanted to take her breasts in his mouth and taste the sweetness of her. He wanted her selfishly and shamelessly and the only difference between now and then was that she no longer trusted him.

He was breathing hard when he forced himself to release her, and the withdrawal was painful. For a moment he kept his eyes closed, afraid to face the accusation and confusion in hers. Bracing his hands against her waist, he stepped away.

Stacey's hands trailed away from his wrists and clenched slowly against her thighs. Inside she was still quivering with the fine wire of unfulfilled need, but she would not flinch from his sober gaze. It had caught her off guard, this sudden passion, but why it should surprise her she did not know. He was the only man who had ever fulfilled her, and the memories of that one night when she had felt free to love were a powerful inducement. There was danger in constant exposure; she had known that. Now they had sexual frustration to add to their list of conflicts and uncertainties.

Jon said quietly, "If you want me to apologize, I will. But I won't mean it." And the lines of his face tightened. "But if you want me to be ashamed of the way I feel I can't. I don't respond only to candlelight and soft moods, and if that makes me less than your perfect dream man I'm sorry. I wanted you a minute ago, and I would have made love to you here on the kitchen floor and I wouldn't have regretted it, but you would have. That's me, Stacey," he added, more gently, "the way I really am. I want you when the time is right and sometimes when it isn't; I want you for the wrong reasons and the right ones, and I guess if that's the worst you have to learn about me, then it's past time you discovered it."

She looked at him—his face still flushed and his eyes intense with desire, the slow, controlled push of his breast muscles against his T-shirt, the lightly tanned arms that were now drawn into unconscious knots of restraint. Her heart wouldn't stop pounding, and her throat was dry. She felt hot and shaky all over just from looking at him, just from knowing that a silent glance, a touch of the hand, a few steps out of the room and they could rediscover the breathless magic that had transported them into a world of make-believe in Boston—but not quite.

Stacey turned away slowly, concentrating her careful attention on the deliberate movements she made to return to normality. She took the plates from the cabinet, the silverware from the drawer. She turned to check the bubbling green beans. She said quietly, "You're probably right."

Her voice was not entirely steady, but it was the best she could do. "I did want to keep it—you—sheltered and protected. Special. I didn't expect you ever to become part of my life because I knew—" She had to clear her throat. She was trying to be as rational as possible. "I knew you didn't belong here. I was afraid it would spoil what we had had."

"And did it?" Jon was not aware of breathing, waiting for her answer.

She looked at him, clearly, evenly. "It's different," she said. Yes, it had been different from the moment she had gone to his apartment in New York. Maybe she had been hoping for something to give her a reason to mistrust him, something that would reassure her there was no way he could ever really belong to her. She did not know, She only knew that there was a grain of mistrust, as childish as it seemed, and that things were no longer perfect between them. Living with him day-to-day had only reinforced the imperfections. This was not the way she wanted it. She had never wanted it this way.

Jon looked at Stacey helplessly, not knowing what to say. What could he say? What right did he have to pressure her about relationships and commitment when he had no intention of offering her either? He did not know what he wanted from her. He did not know anything except that in some way she satisfied a selfish need within him to be a part of something real, and that he could offer her nothing real in return. Each of them was living out fantasies in his own way and they were making a mess of it. She was probably right. He never should have disturbed the status quo.

Jon came to stand behind her, wishing that through a touch or a word he could make everything right between them, wishing that he could tell her what he wanted, and in so doing could open the door for her to want the same thing. He wished it could be easy and uncomplicated between them. Of course, in real life, things rarely were.

Stacey was working at the stove. He was so close she could feel the whisper of his breath, but he did not touch her. Somehow his presence behind her seemed very protecting, almost comforting. She said, concentrating on her work, "Can you eat potatoes?"

"Sure," Jon answered vaguely. "As long as you don't put any"—he watched as she dropped half a stick of margarine into the pot and it began to melt its yellow flavor over the creamy potatoes—"butter in them," he finished lamely.

She looked up at him, and he did not know what else to do but smile at her. He cupped a silky handful of her hair against her neck, and he bent to place a single affectionate kiss on her cheek. The unexpected tenderness of that gesture caused sudden tears to brim in Stacey's eyes, and they were tears of sadness and yearning, of frustration and neglect. Swiftly, with an unsteady breath, he closed those glistening eyes with his lips; he drew her to him.

Her arms came around his waist and he just held her as she held him, quietly, soothingly. He wanted to promise her something then, to give her something or do something for her to erase the hurt that he, in his clumsiness, had caused her. It hurt Jon to see her in pain. It made him angry and disgusted with himself. She was right. He was selfishly using her to satisfy his needs, emotional and physical, and he could give her nothing in return. Women like Stacey needed love and care, protection and permanence. He did not know anything about any of those things. He had already made his choice, but he wanted to play at living in her world. Each of them was looking for something entirely different in the other; none of it was real, and there was no place where they could meet on common ground. There was overwhelming sorrow in the realization.

He touched her chin with his finger; there was shame in the relief he felt that the tears had dried. He looked down at her soberly. "I'll leave tomorrow," he offered quietly, "if you want me to. I didn't mean to complicate your life."

Stacey was surprised at the alarm that shot through her when he said that. She did not want him to leave. If nothing else was clear, that was. She was afraid he would grow bored with her; she was afraid she would begin to expect too much from him; she was afraid of the bleakness in his eyes when he finally realized there was nothing for him here and he said a final good-bye. She was afraid of the time when the pull of his own restlessness drew him back into a world into which she could not follow. But somehow all those fears seemed small and faraway when faced with the present reality of his leaving. "I—I don't want you to," she said quickly, stumbling over the words.

"Are you sure?" he insisted, examining her face anxiously.

She nodded and tucked her face against his shoulder shyly, tightening her arms around him. The relief she had felt when she saw in his eyes that he did not really want to leave, either, was overwhelming. "I guess if you can put up with me a few more days," she mumbled grumpily, "I can put up with you."

A grin of silly relief spread over his face as he ducked his head to look at her, and happiness bubbled up inside him like a clear wellspring. "I'll make a deal with you," he volunteered, squeezing her briefly. "You lighten up on Granny and stop running around like a bellhop at the Waldorf-Astoria, and I'll eat your damn watercress sandwiches without complaint and even stop raiding your cookie jar at night. Fair?"

She giggled and nodded and they held each other. It always seemed when they were in each other's arms, whether in passion or companionship, that fantasy dissolved into warm reality and nothing was really impossible.

Chapter Ten

Stacey was surprised to hear Josie's voice at such an early hour on a morning neither of them had to work. They had all gone out to dinner the night before, gotten in quite late, and Josie, with a mischievous twinkle in her eyes, had glanced at Jon and promised Stacey she wouldn't bother her for the rest of the week. Besides, even though Josie was always up at seven with her kids, whether she had to work or not, she was never so inconsiderate of her friends as to call before noon.

Stacey sat up, pushing her hair out of her eyes and squinting against the morning sun that spilled through her light muslin curtains. "Yeah, Jose," she mumbled. "What's up?"

It was just a little after seven. Jon would already be out running. He had fallen into the habit of making his own breakfast when he returned— fruit and granola—and even putting coffee on for Stacey, so she could sleep late. The shower problem was solved, too. By the time Stacey got yawningly out of bed at nine, Jon was halfway through his day, popping in to say good morning and steal a piece of buttered toast from her plate before he returned to his exercise session in his room, reading the paper, or cutting fresh flowers from the garden. Everything was much calmer, now that they were settling into a routine. Stacey thought that by the time Jon left next week she would have almost gotten used to having him around, and she tried not to think about that. There was no point in borrowing sorrow from the future.

Drowsily Stacey knew something must be wrong, for Josie to call her so early, but it wasn't until she focused on the tone of her friend's voice that real alarm hit. It was tight, a little thick, Stacey knew immediately Josie had been crying. And her request was even more cause for concern. Josie said, "Could I bring the kids over?"

Stacey sat up straighter, dragging her hair into a ponytail at the nape of her neck, her brow creasing. Josie never asked Stacey to baby-sit except in the direst of emergencies; they both worked with children all day long and Josie was not about to impose her own children on Stacey in the evenings. Stacey said automatically, "Sure," and she took her breath for questions which Josie would not allow.

"They may have to spend the night," Josie added. Her voice sounded strange, forcefully controlled and faraway. Stacey knew then that this was no time for prying questions. The best she could do for her friend was give her cooperation and support, and Josie would tell her what was wrong when she was ready. "No problem," Stacey assured her, mentally arranging her day in preparation for the invasion. "Do you want me to come get them?"

"No, no, I'll feed them and get their things together. I'll be over in about an hour."

And that was the only explanation Stacey got.

It was Jon, returning from his run, who greeted Josie when she drove up with the children. Stacey hesitated at the window, thinking surely Josie would come in, but she only unloaded her passengers, put two bags of clothing and necessities into Jon's arms, and was driving off by the time Stacey reached the front walk.

Jon approached her with a quizzical, amused expression on his face, shifting the packages in his arm to awkwardly pat the head of the two-year-old, who immediately started to scream for her mother. Carrie, the oldest, and David, the six-year-old, were too busy chasing a black-and-orange cat through the marigolds to give much heed to their mother's departure.

Stacey, prepared for just such an eventuality, went to the screeching Kim, with a cookie in her hand, and Jon chided mildly above her, "Food bribery. Shame on you; that's very bad psychology." But Kim was quiet now, and they could hear each other talk. "What's going on?" he inquired.

Stacey looked at him helplessly. "Did Josie say anything to you?"

He shook his head. He was sweaty and flushed, his beautiful bright hair pushed away from his face with a stained kerchief, his chest glistening and his shorts dark with damp patches that clung to his skin in places. Stacey almost forgot the question, the subject, the two noisy children in the flower bed and the one sniffling into her cookie, as she looked at him. "I think," Jon offered quietly, mindful of listening ears, "there may be domestic problems."

Stacey moved her eyes from his naked muscular legs to his face, which was sober and concerned. Her heart began to pound with a delayed reaction, and she was irritated with herself for being more concerned about Jon's state of undress than she was with her friend's problems. She apologized quickly, taking Kim's hand as she got to her feet, "I'm sure it won't be for very long. Josie's never done anything like this before. I'll think of something to keep them entertained; they won't be any trouble."

"What, are you kidding?" asked Jon, his eyes lighting with familiar quick enthusiasm. "We'll have a ball!"

There is no day longer, more wearing, or hectic than one spent entertaining another person's children. Stacey was used to it, but not in her own home, on her own time, with two other adults interacting in the ménage. Whether Jon was really enjoying himself or only pretending, Stacey could not be sure, but his patience and adaptability were commendable if nothing else. He kept the children in the backyard most of the day, at Stacey's suggestion, making a tent out of forked sticks and old sheets, allowing himself to be murdered in cold blood, endlessly and without complaint, by a ruthless six-year-old cowboy. He somehow even managed to get nine-year-old Carrie interested in "boys' games" for a while, and he was not above cookie therapy when Kim threatened to whimper. Stacey poured a river of juice into a sinkful of glasses, fixed six different lunches for various tastes and dietary restrictions, and dedicated herself to a two-hour conversation with Carrie about the boys in her class, while Kim napped and Stacey wished she could be doing the same. Mimi was very helpful and there was no doubt that she enjoyed having the children. She was the one who convinced Kim to nap, and later in the afternoon she got Carrie interested in listening to records. But she was also ready for bed at nine o'clock.

Jon was lying on the floor with his hands folded on his chest, having just completed the battle of putting David to bed in his room. The cowboy hat, six sizes too small, was pulled down over his eyes. Stacey had just gotten Kim to sleep in her arms. Stacey's shoulders and back were aching and her arms were numb from holding the baby, but she was too tired to get up and put her into bed with her sister Mimi was simply sitting in her chair, looking exhausted.

"It's amazing," murmured Stacey, but she was too weary to even feel amusement. "Three healthy, capable adults reduced to living corpses by a band of imps half our size." She glanced at Mimi. "Tell me again about the glories of grandmotherhood," she challenged dryly.

Mimi got heavily to her feet, sighing. "Let me think about it overnight. Maybe over the weekend. Or better yet, check with me sometime next year. Good night one and all," she paused to declare graciously. "We shall live to fight another day."

Jon was smilig as he called good night to her, and he sat up reluctantly. He looked at Stacey for a moment in frank exhaustion. "I am worn out," he admitted. "I bet I'll actually sleep eight hours tonight."

"Why don't you go on to bed?" Stacey suggested. "I'm going to, in a minute."

"No, I'll give the cowboy a chance to doze off first. Otherwise he might shoot me for a common horse thief." And he smiled a little reflectively. "Funny thing, I didn't think kids played cowboys anymore. Am I that much out of step?"

"He's addicted to the reruns on local television," Stacey yawned. She blinked to clear her eyes and smiled at him. "It was nice of you to share your bed."

Jon shrugged. "I remember being six years old. Things can get pretty scary." And then he looked at Stacey soberly. "I think he's afraid his daddy won't be home when he goes back. Maybe he hung around me all day as some sort of substitute."

Stacey nodded, worried. The children had hinted of a fight between their parents, but they evidently did not know what it was about. Josie and Carl were very discreet around the children, and the very fact that the children knew anything at all of the trouble was evidence of its seriousness. Stacey found it hard to believe that this could be anything more than a misunderstanding that would surely be cleared up by morning. Josie and Carl had been so happily married for so long, it was inconceivable that anything could gravely threaten their life together.

Jon was sensitive to her concern and did not voice his own speculation. He merely got to his feet and volunteered, "Let me put the little one to bed for you. She looks as though she's out for the night."

Stacey stirred reluctantly, muffling a sigh. "No, I'd better do it. She wears diapers overnight."

Jon looked at her with patient mockery. "Those white plastic things with the tapes on the corners? I was wondering what they were." He scooped Kim gently out of Stacey's arms. "I can manage," he told her, and Stacey was too weary and too grateful to argue with him.

When Jon returned a few minutes later, Stacey was exactly as he had left her, absently rubbing her aching arms. "One diaper securely in place upon one sleeping child," he announced. "Now I can put my head in your lap. Or," he offered as he sat down beside her on the sofa, "maybe it should be the other way around."

Stacey laughed tiredly as he drew her against his shoulder. It was a warm, natural gesture, and it felt good to rest against him for a time. "We'll alternate," she suggested. "How did you learn about diapers, anyway?"

"I have a couple of nieces," he said. "I don't get to see them as often as I'd like, but they used to wear diapers."

Again Stacey laughed, weakly and comfortably.

"This day," she mused, "was a disaster. A certifiable disaster."

"Oh, it wasn't that bad," he objected, though without a great deal of enthusiasm. "I think we made pretty good surrogate parents on such short notice. It was kind of fun, in a kinky sort of way."

Surrogate parents. That was exactly what they had been doing—playing house, pretending to be a family, Jon playing cowboys in the backyard, Stacey wiping noses and being a confidante for a preadolescent. Sure, it was fun. Because it was only make-believe.

Stacey sat up a little straighter, dreading the walk upstairs and the sharing of her bed with two little girls. As though reading her mind, Jon suggested, "Why don't you stretch out here for a while? There's room for both of us."

"You should go to bed," she murmured, but it was an irresistible temptation to lower her head onto the sofa cushion and uncurl her tired legs.

Jon drew her bare feet into his lap. "In a minute."

He absently began to stroke her ankles, and there was nothing erotic about the gesture—it was simply comfortable and comforting, as though they really were part of a long-standing family, husband and wife who had grown used to one another, relaxing together at the end of a mutually exhausting day. There was warmth in that image, and a great temptation to carry it further, and under other circumstances, Stacey probably would have enjoyed maintaining the illusion. But she couldn't help thinking about Josie and Carl.

The truth was a harsh contrast to the game she and Jonathon and Mimi had played all day, and Stacey shifted her weight and frowned a little, disturbed.

Jon sensed her change of mood. "Worried about Josie?" he inquired sympathetically.

Stacey nodded. "It's just so strange. I know I have no right to burden them with my faith in the entire institution of marriage, but I've always thought they had the perfect marriage—living proof that the whole thing could work, you know? Oh, sure, they've had their problems, but working them out was what made them stronger. And now, I don't know." Again she frowned. "It just seems as though, if they had the perfect marriage and it didn't work, then there's no reason for anyone else to try." She lifted her shoulders lightly. "I know it sounds silly."

Jon did not appear to think it was silly. "I don't see too many people getting married anymore. Sometimes they live together, but even that doesn't last very long. Of course it's different in the theater." As he well knew. One couldn't expect to have a relationship when self-satisfaction was the prime motivation, and neither party could distinguish reality from illusion. And then he smiled at her. "But you can't condemn the entire institution to failure because of a few very human examples of it. At least Josie and her husband had the courage to try. Besides"—he began to massage her feet with easy, gentle strokes—"they may work it out."

The deft movements of Jon's skilled fingers on

the balls of Stacey's feet felt incredibly good. Tension and fatigue began to fade with each movement, from the tips of her toes upward along her legs. "Umm," she murmured and closed her eyes, "that feels marvelous."

"I know. Zone therapy. There are nerves in the feet that relate to each zone of the body, and massaging them can relax the whole body." He hesitated. "Did you ever think about it, Stacey? Having a family, children?"

She opened her eyes. She was too relaxed from the soothing manipulation of Jon's fingers to feel threatened by the question. And besides, from the look on Jon's face, it was purely a rhetorical one. "Who doesn't? But I don't know. I work with children all day, and they are my family. I suppose I might love children of my own better, but it's hard to imagine now. I guess," she added, "before I got into special education, I used to daydream about children of my own, and maybe that's why I chose the profession I did. It satisfies my maternal instincts." She turned the question to him. "What about you?"

Jon smiled vaguely. "I always thought I would make a good father." But, of course, that, too, was only a daydream. "I had a nice childhood."

"I didn't." Stacey closed her eyes again. "My father was an alcoholic and my mother was a victim. I used to spend hours in my room, listening to them fight"—the tightening of her lips was both sad and derisive—"dreaming I was adopted, and that my real parents would drive up to the door in a shiny white Cadillac and rescue me."

She hoped Jon would not try to analyze that. She knew perfectly well that a childhood spent dreaming for better things was the reason she had rushed into a marriage too illusory to last, and why even now she could not deal with life's imperfections. They frightened her.

Jon did not need to voice his understanding, and for that Stacey was grateful. Both of them were still living out their childhood, he supposed. He by returning to the world of make-believe every night on stage, and she by employing the same techniques in everyday life that she had used to escape an unhappy childhood. Perhaps that was the only thing they had ever had in common. He did not want to think that was true.

Stacey felt relaxed and weightless, yet energized and renewed as he worked his magic from the tips of her toes to the bottoms of her heels, gently rotating tense ankles, stroking the tops of her feet to quivering, tingling life. His touch was electric and soothing, skilled and deliberate, druggingly caressing. And as the fatigue drained from her taut muscles she was drawn into a new awareness of him, the power and the comfort of him, the wonder of his touch and the need to have him close. She could hear the soft sound of his breathing and feel the intensity of his eyes upon her, and as his fingertips paused, encircling her ankles, the moment was subtly changed.

Very slowly, very lightly, she could feel the caressing motions of his fingers slide upward along her smooth bare shin, moving downward to massage and stroke her calf. Lethargy and content-

ment awoke to a new pleasure charged with wel-
coming desire, and her pliant muscles responded
to the quickening and the tensing of his. Stacey
could feel dancing, evocative fingers tracing path-
ways over her calves and shins. She could hear the
rustle of springs as he shifted his weight and
leaned over her, feel the warm quickening of his
breath as he bent to place slow, flowering kisses
on each place his fingers touched. His heat fell
over her, his presence covered her, as his hands
and lips moved upwards, gathering her rounded
calves and gently separating them for the touch of
his lips, sending hot, moist shivers through her as
his mouth covered her kneecaps one by one, trail-
ing her flesh upward beneath the path of his
fingers toward the hem of her shorts. And then
his lips were against the soft flesh of her inner
thigh, electrifying her, mesmerizing her, letting
her drown within the sensation, making her want
him, need him, ache to be a part of him and to
make it last forever. To make it real.

Jon touched her cheek; Stacey opened her eyes.
His smile was gentle, but there was something
strange within his eyes—an intensity, a question,
a reluctance. "It's late," he said, "and I think
you're about to doze off on me. Better get to
bed."

Stacey blinked and smiled and sat up to say
good night.

It had all been nothing more than a daydream.

Josie came at nine o'clock the next morning to
pick up the children. The timing was perfect. The

children were fed and dressed and packed and had not yet had a chance to start worrying about their mother; just as Stacey was trying to prepare some way to distract them when they did become restless, Josie drove up.

She looked pale and worn, and the puffiness of her eyes was from more than a sleepless night. She greeted the children with buoyant enthusiasm, but it was only a disguise for her silent distress. Stacey hovered anxiously, knowing Josie now wanted to talk, but couldn't do it in the presence of the children. Jon picked up the signal immediately and volunteered to take each of them on a puttering ride around the backyard on his motorcycle if their mother agreed. Under normal circumstances Josie would never have given her permission, and it alarmed Stacey that she did so without hesitation now. Mimi went out to supervise and left Stacey and Josie alone in the kitchen.

Josie watched them from the window as the background sound of a chugging engine and excited children floated through. "He's a jewel, isn't he?" she said absently. "Something really special." She turned to Stacey with an absent smile. "Anything particularly interesting going on between you two?"

Stacey carefully followed her lead, pouring two cups of coffee and setting them on the table. "No. We're getting along a lot better than I expected, I suppose. I think he really enjoyed having the children around." She gave a dry smile. "It's a break from his usual routine."

"You sound as though that's bad." Josie obviously wanted to escape from her own problems for a while, and Stacey cooperated. They sat down at the table.

"He enjoys being here," Stacey said. "And I"—she lowered her eyes briefly to her cup to hide the depth of emotion that verified her words—"I enjoy being with him. But it's nothing permanent."

Josie said quietly, sipping her coffee, "What is?"

"Oh, Josie." Stacey could stand it no longer. She reached for her friend's hand, her face creased with anxiety and concern. "What is it? What happened?"

Josie took a deep breath and set her cup on the saucer with only a brief clatter. She pushed back a handful of wispy curls and even managed a semblance of a tight smile. "What else?" she declared. "Another woman."

Stacey felt as though someone had just bludgeoned her in the chest with a feather pillow; had it been her own husband she could not have been more shocked. She actually felt the breath leave her lungs. "But—but I can't believe it!" she gasped. "I—not Carl! Are you sure?" And she saw the agony deep within her friend's eyes, and she knew it was true. There was no mistake.

"Surely," Stacey began carefully, still trying to adjust to the revelation, "it was just one of those things, a one-night stand. It couldn't have meant anything, Josie." This was she, Stacey, saying these things after she had suffered so over Jon's faithlessness? Jon, who owed her no loyalty, but had readily admitted that his relationship with the other woman was meaningless—Stacey had not been so quick to forgive him. How could she in conscience advise her friend to forgive a disloyal husband?

And Josie shook her head slowly, not meeting Stacey's eyes. "It was a one-night stand that lasted over a year," she said heavily.

Josie withdrew her hand and stood up, moving around the room in short, tightly controlled steps that tried to disguise her agitation. "She was married, too," Josie said. "The bitch." Her voice broke and she took a breath, turning away from Stacey, dragging her hand through her hair, tilting her face toward the ceiling for a few steadying breaths. "Damn it," she said lowly. "I am not going to cry. I'm finished with crying."

Stacey sat there, aching for Josie, furious and horrified by Carl, not knowing what to do. In a moment, more in control of herself, Josie finished, "She didn't even leave me the satisfaction of thinking Carl had come back to me of his own choice." The small sound of incredulity and disgust she made could have been a choked laugh or a smothered sob. "She went back to her own husband, and Carl had no place else to go. And do you know"—she turned to Stacey, her eyes filled with a mixture of amazement, self-derision, and even a small amount of amusement—"the incredible thing is that all this time I didn't suspect a thing. He was leading two lives and I didn't have a hint. I never would have known," she pondered in slow, angry incredulity, "if I hadn't found the good-bye note. It could all have been over and I never would have known a thing.''

Silence echoed on Josie's choked, startled breath, and she stood, staring at Stacey as though she had only for the first time realized the truth of what she had said. "I would have never known," she repeated dully. "But that wouldn't have made it any less real." She turned slowly away. "Maybe it's better this way."

In the backyard the sounds of Jon's laughter mixed with the children's over the low background sputter of the engine. Automatically Stacey turned her head toward the sound.

"Yes," Josie decided with a breath. "It's always better to face the truth. Then you can deal with it."

Josie came back to the table and even managed a brave, if rather wan, smile. She sat down and took up her coffee again.

Stacey had to know. She asked quietly, "What are you going to do?"

Josie did not answer for a time. She sipped her coffee, her gaze directed toward the sound of the revelry in the backyard. Then she lowered her cup to the saucer and she looked at Stacey calmly. "I'm going to take him back," she said matter-of-factly. "Forgive him. Try to start over."

Stacey did not know whether she was relieved or horrified. How could Josie do that? The perfect marriage had been irrevocably tainted, and how could they just go on, pretending nothing had happened?

Josie shrugged, reading the confusion in her

friend's eyes. "I know. It won't ever be the same." There was bitterness in the tightening of her lips, hardness in her eyes. "We've lost something very precious, and there's no way to get it back. I'll probably never trust him again; I'll never be able to forget. I'll never feel the same way about him again, knowing that he doesn't feel the same about me. But he still loves me, in his way, and he wants to try again." Now her expression faded into a hint of a smile that was almost overwhelmed by the sorrow in her eyes. "And I'm going to take him back because that's what you do when you love someone. You do the best you can. It's called real life; nothing is ever perfect."

Stacey reached for her friend's hand and simply held it. She did not know what else to do.

Chapter Eleven

Stacey had been watching Jon from the window off and on for an hour before she decided to go outside and join him. He had been working on his bike, and there was something fascinating about watching a man who was so gracefully ethereal onstage apply himself to such a mundane chore. There were only three days remaining before he must leave, but sometimes Stacey still found herself looking at him and almost believing she was dreaming. He just did not seem to belong here.

When she looked back on the past two weeks she was quietly amazed by the changes that had subtly taken place. Somehow he had become a part of her life, fitting into her routine, making his presence easy and natural. She was used to seeing him at the breakfast table, accustomed to the presence of his shaving kit in the bathroom, comfortable with the sound of his voice in the evenings. They still had their disagreements. She still went around turning off lights behind him, and he still gave her reproving looks when he thought she was being too protective of Mimi, but even that had become part of the routine. They had their quiet times; they had stimulating conversations, but they were hardly ever alone. And it was only when Stacey looked back on their first meeting and the time before that when he had been only a fantasy figure to her that she was struck by that feeling of unreality, as though this couldn't possibly be happening. Jon Callan could not really be polishing his motorcycle in her backyard. Jon Callan belonged on the stage, bringing thousands of fantasies to life, and the protective feelings Stacey was beginning to develop for him frightened her. In three more days he would go back where he belonged, and Stacey would remain here in her own world, and she did not like to think about what the future held for them.

Jon looked up when she came out, grinning as he indicated the fresh wax job. "Not bad, huh?"

Stacey shielded her eyes against the glare in an exaggerated gesture. "Positively breathtaking."

He tossed the polishing cloth into the nearby trash can and suggested enthusiastically, "Let's take it for a spin and show it off."

Stacey laughed. "Be my guest."

"Coward," he taunted.

"Better a live coward than a —"

"This, from the woman who braved security guards and stagehands and a live audience to send a trysting note to a complete stranger?"

Stacey had never thought there would come a day when they could joke about their first meeting, or that she would be able to confess the truth about it. But so many barriers had been broken down between them, simply in the course of their day-to-day acquaintance, that the magic of their first encounter had lost a lot of its glitter. In a way, that was comfortable.

The sun colored her cheeks as she lowered her eyes shyly. Her hair was fastened on either side of her face in pigtails and it caught the glint of the bright afternoon; in shorts, moccasins, and a modest button-down shirt she looked young and vulnerable and, to Jon, utterly embraceable. She said, "Jonathon, there's something you should know about that note." She looked at him, her eyes sun-clear but emotionally opaque. It was a fascinating combination. "I never intended to send it to you. I almost died of embarrassment when Josie stole it from me and gave it to that security guard. I think I would have left the theater if I could have found the nerve."

He laughed, caressing her shoulder with his hand briefly and companionably. "I think I always suspected as much. I never could quite resolve that act of daring with the prim and proper young woman you turned out to be. Remind me to thank Josie next time I see her."

She lifted her eyebrows in a mocking challenge. "Prim and proper?"

"Bad choice of words," he conceded with an abashed grin, and Stacey wondered if he, too, was thinking of the way that first encounter had ended. *That* he considered prim? What did he expect from someone "wild"? The heat that tingled through her with this course of thought bore no relation to the summer afternoon and was not entirely unpleasant. "Let's just say," Jon amended politely, "that you're not much of a risk taker."

Stacey looked at him, so beautiful and solid before her with his fiery bright hair and dancing electric eyes, the golden honey tan he had acquired over the past two weeks, and the way his perfect body was molded into a casual T-shirt and jeans. No, Stacey did not take risks. But Jon had risked coming here to be with her, risked rejection and exposure and disappointment. Stacey felt that that should tell her something fundamental about the differences between them, but she was not certain what.

She glanced at the motorcycle. "How fast does that thing go?"

"As fast as I want it to." Then Jon grinned and turned to take a helmet from the travel trunk. "Not fast at all," he assured her.

"But I don't have a—"

He stopped her by slipping the heavy black and red helmet over her hair.

She looked at him skeptically. "Do you always carry an extra for passengers?"

He endured the thinly disguised jealousy with a patient smile as he fastened the chin strap. "No passengers," he informed her. "I bought this for you, just the other day."

"What if I had said no?"

"I felt safe in my investment," Jon returned, pulling the other helmet over his head. "Mimi has already volunteered to take your place. Now there's nothing to it," he reassured her as he straddled the bike and waited for her to do the same. "Just hold on to me and lean into the turns. You're going to love it."

"Don't go fast," Stacey pleaded, and winced and tightened her arms around his waist as the machine roared to life.

For the first few miles Stacey wrapped her arms around him in a paralyzing grip, squeezing her eyes closed, wondering what madness had possessed her. The warm wind stung her bare legs and the smells of diesel and asphalt filled her nostrils as the thunder of the engine blocked out even the sound of her own thoughts. The speed limit was forty-five miles per hour, but she felt as though they were exceeding it by twice as much. She was far from loving it.

Perhaps it was simply immunity by exposure, or perhaps she began to feel more comfortable once they left the traffic behind for seldom-traveled country roads—or it was possibly because her aching arms simply could not maintain their death-grip any longer—but Stacey gradually began to relax. She opened her eyes. It wasn't as bad as she expected. The green meadows and tree-lined roads were larger than life, brilliantly colored, and clearly visible as she and Jon passed them at a leisurely pace. When she lifted her face, the breeze brought the scent of grass and wildflowers, and the sun felt good against her skin. The heavy vehicle absorbed the bumps and ridges in the road, and the padded seat was comfortable. And it felt good to be pressed against Jon, her chest against his back, her thighs surrounding his, her fingers curling around his belt. It was an intimacy that hinted of eroticism, with all the pleasures and none of the threats.

Jon turned and shouted something to her. His voice was carried away by the wind but he was grinning, so Stacey smiled and nodded back enthusiastically. To her very great surprise she was enjoying it. Had there ever been a time, even to the limits of her imagination, when she could foresee herself riding on the back of a motorcycle with Jon Callan in her arms? Sometimes truth was even better than fiction.

He slowed the engine; Stacey hung on tightly as he made a careful turn off the road onto what barely seemed to be a path between undergrowth and wild shrubbery, covered by flattened grass that grew tall on either side of their wheels. "I wanted to show you this," Jon shouted to her. They were barely moving now, which was good, because the path was bumpy and jolting, and Stacey could hear what he said. "I discovered this just the other day. These"—he gestured to the worn down grass ahead of them—"are my tracks."

After a while the narrow, worn trail he was following gave way to a larger grassless area that could have been a gully or a dried up creek bed or an old road. Only clumps of grass survived here and there along the course of hard-packed dirt as they moved into a shadowy canopy of trees and climbing vines. The air here was cool and fresh, smelling of all the rich tones of the forest, with a slight dampness to it that indicated water nearby. The sun came through in patches to illuminate the dusty road, and swarms of gossamer insects moved before them. Then Jon lifted his arm, and Stacey followed his gaze to what he had brought her here to see.

It was a very old bridge, out in the middle of nowhere, its weather-darkened wood sagging and crumbling. Parts of it had fallen away entirely, but it still formed a complete, though obviously unsafe, span over what must once have been a sizeable waterway. Broken supports stretching upward gave evidence of intricate craftsmanship and an age beyond this century. It was starkly beautiful, sitting there immune to the threats of the encroaching forest, enduring long after it had served its purpose.

The engine died and silence echoed over the scurrying and chirping sounds of the wooded countryside. They removed their helmets while Jon balanced the weight of the motorcycle with his feet, and he said, "I think it used to be a covered bridge. There aren't too many of them standing anymore, are there? But it's just sat out here, all these years, forgotten."

He took her hand as they went to explore, and Stacey grew excited as he pointed out to her the workmanship, the wooden pegs and iron spikes used in place of nails, and they speculated on where this road must once have led and how old the bridge was. The course of the river or creek it once had spanned had apparently been diverted, for at the bottom of the grassy banks that sloped deeply was only a clear, bubbling stream, decorated by flat stepping-stones and smooth white pebbles. "This," declared Stacey, sinking down onto the fragrant grassy bank, "is like a child's fairy story. The *Secret of the Woods*. Do you think anyone else has ever been here?"

"Not this year," Jon assured her. He was tugging off his boots, and at Stacey's questioning look he returned gravely, "Would any two self-respecting characters in a children's story be able to resist wading in that creek?"

Stacey giggled and kicked off her moccasins, racing him down the bank. Though the day was hot, the ankle-deep water was a shock, and it was refreshing for only a minute. Stacey's squeals and Jon's laughter rose above the still forest sounds, sending squirrels into angry chattering and birds into noisy flight, as Jon couldn't resist kicking and splashing the cold water at her. At last, shivering, Stacey made her escape to a patch of sun on the bank beneath the old bridge and she collapsed there, breathing deeply of the earth-spiced air, squinting her eyes at the patches of blue and white beneath the framework of the bridge.

Jon lay on his stomach beside her, and the warmth of the sun and the cushion of grass were as comfortable as the silence between them. Stacey had expected to be sore and tired after her first experience with a motorcycle, for they had ridden quite a way, but she was surprised to feel no effects at all. The bike was just as comfortable as Jon had said it was.

"It's funny," she mused, half smiling into the lacework of sun that was scattered over her face. "I never would have pictured you on a motorcycle."

Jon turned over lazily, linking his hands behind his head. "Part of my macho image," he confessed. "You learn to develop all sorts of masculine badges in my profession."

She glanced at him. "It must have been hard on you, growing up," she realized with sudden insight. "I'll bet the other kids gave you a rough time."

He shrugged agreement. "It could have been worse if I had let it be," he admitted. "When I got tired of my brothers defending me all the time, I took up karate." He grinned. "Then I could defend them. Needless to say I wasn't the most popular kid in school. It's a wonder I grew up as normally as I did."

She smiled, lightly brushing a curious ladybug off the front of his shirt. "There's nothing normal about you at all."

"Since you wouldn't stand a chance if I decided to show off my karate skills," he murmured, his eyes half-closed, "I'll take that as a compliment."

Stacey smiled, and when she turned her face to avoid the glare of the sun her cheek brushed his shoulder. Jon unfolded his arm to curve around the top of her head, his fingers resting against her arm.

"You have ugly feet," Stacey noticed absently.

"I know. It's the curse of the dancer."

She lifted her face to look at him. "I suppose you're anxious to get back to work."

Jon could not lie to her about that. He did miss it; it was his life. He missed the physical exertion, the sense of accomplishment, the beauty of performing his art. He missed the challenges and the triumphs, and he missed the applause. But he would miss this, too, the quiet times, the little chores, the absence of tension and worry—Stacey, being with her, relaxing with her. It made his throat tighten when he thought how much he would miss her. These past weeks with her had not been perfect; they had not been all he had imagined or wanted, but they had still, in some way, been what he had needed. And because their time together had not been entirely perfect, it was all the more precious; it would leave him wanting more. And he did not know what to do about it.

"Yes," he admitted. "I need to be working. But this has been good for me."

Stacey absently plucked a blade of grass, drawing it between her fingers with a soft squeaking sound. "Do you still feel like packing it all in?"

He laughed softly and shifted his weight to draw her head on his shoulder; she settled comfortably against him. "That's a chronic condition. I think it has something to do with age." She glanced at him curiously and he explained, "I'll be thirty—" Then he grinned and amended, "We'll be thirty in a few months. I hate to break it to you, Stace, but the body starts to go around then, and there's not a thing you can do about it. I can't dance forever."

She had never thought about that. Jon Callan, not dancing—it was a shock. She stared at him. "But what will you do?"

Jon did not seem a fraction as concerned as she was. "I'd like to have my own company, of course," he replied. "Choreograph, maybe do a few special appearances. It's the touring that's killing me."

"But, surely," she ventured, her brows knotting in slow assimilation of all this information, "you could do that now if you wanted to."

He shook his head slowly. "I don't have that kind of money. And the backers who approach me now aren't interested in the kind of company I want to form."

"Which is?" she inquired curiously.

"Avant-garde and improvisational," he answered immediately. "A lot like Elements, only with more exposure for the unknown and just-getting-started dancers. That's why," he confessed, "I'm going to have to resign myself to Maalox and life on the road for another couple of years. I want to build up the dancers' reputation and my own and learn as much as I can, so that when the time comes, the right backers will come to me with hats in hand."

She smiled, absently tracing a light pattern over his hazel-flecked hand where it fell across her shoulder. "You won't have any trouble at all," she assured him. "You worry too much."

"That, too, is a chronic condition."

"Won't you miss it?" she wanted to know. "The excitement of the performance, the approval of your audience . . . dancing?"

"I suppose," he admitted reflectively. And then his smile was wry. "I won't miss the starvation or the sweat or the stage fright."

Stacey shook her head in slow amazement. "I

don't understand you. What do you, Jon Callan, a legend in his own time, have to be frightened about?"

"Failing, mostly," he answered her seriously. "Disappointing my audience. Doing something wrong, dropping my partner or hurting someone. Falling," he admitted at last, with an almost bashful quirk of his lips, "I'm terrified of falling."

She looked at him, and beyond her amazement at his truthful chronicle of his weakness there was sincerity in her eyes. She was deeply moved. "You've never done any of those things," she reminded him. "You've never failed."

"No," he agreed. "Not yet." Then he turned to her, lightly smoothing the ruffle of her bangs with his fingers, and he smiled. "You're the best cure for stage fright I've ever found, do you know that?" he said, and his eyes twinkled. "A very interestingly packaged tranquilizer. Take one kiss before each show"—he dropped his lips teasingly over hers—"and two afterwards." Two more swift, nibbling kisses, and he looked at her, his eyes light and warm. She smiled back, reaching up to touch his hair, and he kissed her again, with tenderness and lingering affection, slowly and lazily, as though they had all the time in the world. Then he traced the curve of her smile with his fingers, his face soft and content, and he turned his head to rest on the grass again.

They lay beside one another, listening to the twittering of the birds and the bubbling of the creek, the warm stillness of the day invading their bloodstreams like a subtle opiate.

It was a long time later that Jon asked lazily, "What are you thinking about?"

"The clouds," answered Stacey, her eyes directed dreamily upwards. "The patterns they make—knights, and ladies and haunted towers, moats and meadows." She smiled. "Castles in the air."

He shifted his weight to lower her head on the grass, propping himself up on one elbow above her. Her eyes reflected the patterns of sky and cloud as clearly as a mountain stream. He rested one hand on her waist as he bent to kiss her.

Stacey received him as naturally as the earth received the sun, curving upward to taste his sweetness. She slipped her hands beneath his shirt and felt the warm smoothness of his back. She did not wonder what it would be like to be undressed by him in the full light of day, in sight of the sun and the wild forest creatures. She felt no shame or fear at the prospect of sharing herself with him, nor did intrusive thoughts of emotional consequences penetrate. Stacey was wrapped in the glow of Jon's presence and compelled by a power greater than logic. She let him guide her.

Jon's hand trailed slowly over her hip and downward to where the cuff of her shorts met warm bare flesh as he took her underlip gently, playfully, between his teeth. He felt the underside of her leg as she curved her knee upward to his caress; he tasted her tongue as it danced over his. The desire that flowed downward and heated his thighs was slow and golden; it began in his heart and spread outward to his body. His fingers brushed the inside of her thighs and felt them loosen and separate to his touch. He drank of her warmth. He wanted to feel her surrounding him, embracing him, covering him; he wanted to be inside her and belong to her. He loved the feel of her hands on his back, caressing his waist, dipping against the band of his belt.

He lifted his face and looked down at her. Through a haze of pleasure and wonder her face was soft and flushed with his kisses, her eyes clear and open. Her smile was dazed and welcoming, and so was his. He tasted the silkiness of her lashes and the delicate hollow beneath her eyes. He unsnapped the catch of her shorts and slipped his hand inside, gently cupping her warmth, feeling her yield to the tender explorations of his fingers.

For Stacey there were no fireworks, no explosions of passion, no wild soarings to the fringes of ecstasy. It was a gentle coupling, slow and warm and lovely, a sharing of minds and bodies and natures. Golden kisses danced off their faces and sweet smiles were exchanged, and Stacey watched Jon's face above her, glorying in his pleasure, touching with her lips each changing expression, loving him. Without the blindness of the depths of passion, she experienced the marvel of shared intimacy, of knowing him and having him close, of giving to him and pleasuring him. When his peak had been reached and surpassed, he did not leave her; he turned on his side and drew her with him, cupping her with his arms and legs. Their bodies still joined, they lay together in the bright splash of sunlight before all the world, stroking and kissing each other, holding each other. In real life the magic did not come every time. There was wonder in the discovery. There were things deeper and more solid than the ephemeral satisfaction of physical love. Jon had never felt more real to her. And Stacey had never loved him more.

Chapter Twelve

Jon was leaving tomorrow. Already he had stayed a day longer than he had planned, so that he would have to make the trip back without stopping, in order to be on time for rehearsals on Monday. Stacey lay in the suspended comfort of her water bed with her arm around his waist and her legs entwined with his, and she smiled a little when she thought of how they had gotten here.

Stacey was not consciously aware that the change in their relationship over the past few days was visible to the untrained eye, but she should have known better. During the day they passed their time much as usual, laughing together, playing together, sharing easy silences and unspoken thoughts, as they always had. The three of them had spent Jon's last evening with them watching television—Jon stretched out on the sofa, Stacey sitting on the floor at his feet, Mimi working a string-art kit on a card table drawn up before the television set.

When the late news came on, Mimi put away her craft work and announced that she was going to bed, then added without blinking an eye, "You two had best do the same—together, if you don't mind. Those stairs make an awful noise when someone tries to sneak up or down them."

Stacey hadn't known whether to gasp in horror or dissolve into a confusion of blushes and giggles, and, in fact, she was too stunned to do either. It was Jon whose shoulders were shaking as they watched her leave the room, and when they were alone he could restrain himself no longer; he burst into laughter, which Stacey could not help joining. So they had walked up the stairs hand-in-hand and gotten into bed beside one another as though it were something they had been doing all their lives, as though they should be doing it for the rest of their lives.

Jon had shown her the magic again in the past three nights. He had shown the delights and variations of making love, the secrets of physical intimacy that only they could know, with a ceaseless thirst for discovery and undaunted drive for adventure that Stacey quickly learned to share. There was quiet, soothing love and there was hard, passionate love. There was warmth and there was heated blindness; there was playfulness and intensity. And there was a special unity they shared in rhythm and unspoken signals, a wonder in the natural way they gave to each other while receiving fulfillment of their own needs. Jon opened her to all of it. He made her feel as though they were the only two people in the world who knew this special compatibility, this magic relationship.

She had been deliberately postponing an examination of her feelings about his leaving. Stacey had known this day would come. She had guessed that it would be painful, but she had not imagined how painful. She had not intended to let him get this close.

For a few days, a short period out of his life and hers, he had taken on mortal form and come to dwell with her. He had visited her real world and become a part of her real life. But, as with all gods in all myths, he must eventually resume his true identity. Jon did not belong here; he did not belong to her. Stacey had always known that.

She did not try to see beyond the time of his departure; she did not reach into the future to imagine what would become of them. There was nothing for them in the future. Like Josie, she had compromised what she wanted with what she could have; she had chosen to have him for a little while, which was all he could offer. She did not pretend it could last, or that it was real. Snatched moments of fantasy—his or hers—were all that would ever be available to them. She could not ask for more. She just had not expected it to hurt so much.

Jon lay with his fingers spread over her stomach, staying still and breathing quietly so he would not disturb her. His eyes were focused on the lacy patterns of moonlight, sifting through the branches of an oak, that were reflected on the ceiling. Her skin felt warm and satiny beneath his fingers, still a little damp from their recent lovemaking. He ached inside when he thought about leaving her.

What had he expected when he came here? A chance to relax, to put his life in perspective, to be with someone who made him feel real and important, someone who understood him. Not sex. Sex was cheap; only with Stacey did it become mystical. Yet sex, too, had come naturally, just as it had that first night, and each time it was more wonderful. Each time it confused him more.

He wondered if she would become pregnant. Jon had never thought about that with any other woman before; perhaps because he had known subconsciously he didn't have to. None of the sleek, ambitious women he knew would bear a child, whether it were his or anyone else's. But Stacey was different. A sense of awe came over him when he thought of his genes mixing with hers, cells joining and dividing and performing miracles because she and he had come together. He had never had such thoughts before.

He could ask her, he supposed. He probably should have done so before now; yet he had deliberately avoided talking about consequences, present or future. He was not sure whether he was afraid of or hoping for an affirmative answer.

He frowned a little when he thought about the conversation he had had with Mimi earlier in the day. In her blunt, bright-eyed way, she had declared, "So, you're leaving us, Jonny. I must say, I'm disappointed in you."

Jon had already sensed that the conversation was not going to be to his advantage, so he only gave her a puzzled smile.

"I was hoping," she explained patiently, as to

one intellectually deficient, "that you would find a way to take my granddaughter with you and leave me in peace."

Jon could not be entirely sure she was teasing, so he played it safe. He directed her attention away from himself and forestalled questions he knew he could not answer. "I want you to tell me something," he challenged, settling himself on a kitchen stool as he watched her peel potatoes for the evening meal. The roles were reversed for once, and Stacey was in the garden, safely out of hearing. "You're a bright young lady—"

Mimi flashed him a brilliant, mocking smile.

"—and perfectly capable of taking care of yourself. You've done nothing but tell me these past few weeks that you want to get rid of this place and move to a retirement village. So why do you let Stacey treat you like an invalid? You play along with her. You let her make your decisions for you. Do you really think that's good for either of you?"

Mimi did not have to think long about her answer. "Good heavens, Jonny," she laughed, "you make it sound so complicated. It's really very simple. Of course, Stacey would be better off out on her own with people her own age—I know that. And, of course, I would be much happier leading my own life. But love is a commitment that does not always allow us a great many options. She stays with me because she loves me and she thinks I need her; I let her pretend she's needed here because I love her. We both make little sacrifices, I guess, and sometimes we make the wrong choices, but those are the things you do for someone you love. That's just the way it is,'' she summed up with a pragmatic confidence that was nonetheless poignant.

Jon had thought about that a lot, and he still did not understand it. The commitment to love was a conscious decision, a dedication, just as was the commitment to art or to any other great calling. It required all of you for all time, and it was not something that could just come along haphazardly and take over your life without warning. It could be accepted or rejected at will. But once accepted, it ruled you completely. Why would anyone want to do something like that to his or her life? It was just too complicated. What he felt for Stacey—need, kinship, tenderness, yearning—were all powerful emotions, but in control. He would have liked to love her, but he had already made his choice.

Jon did not know what would happen when he went back to New York. He couldn't imagine what it would be like without her. He wanted to be able to talk to her every day, to make love to her at night; he wanted her to hold his hand before a performance and wipe his brow afterwards; he wanted to know she would always be there. It was selfish. He knew that. Could he ask her to come on the road with him, to give up her life in favor of his, when he had nothing to offer her in return? It was what he wanted to do, and he knew that would be using her. Stacey was too idealistic, too old-fashioned and genuine to be content with modernistic compromises. He had never said words of love to her. He would not say them without meaning them, yet it grated on his conscience because he gladly would take all the love she had to offer him. But Stacey needed something real from him; she needed promises and strong emotion and total commitment. She knew he was incapable of giving her that. He could not divide himself in two. But he could not ask any more from her without giving something in return.

He could accept the position that had been offered him with the Boston Ballet. At least, then, they could see one another more often. He did not want to join the Boston Ballet. He wanted to stay with Elements and pursue his dream. Selfishly, determinedly, with room for Stacey only on the outskirts of his life. He had already made his choice. Then why did it hurt so much?

Jon turned his head to look at Stacey, carefully, so that only a slight wave of motion was generated. Her eyes were open, and she smiled at him. A slow wave of yearning built within him that was like a steadily consuming fire as he stroked her cheek, and all his rational resolution was plunged into confusion again. He almost asked her, right then, regardless of her needs or desires, to come with him, to leave her life behind and just be there for him when he needed her. He did not know what he wanted anymore, or what was possible or what was right. He only knew that for one more night, one last time, he had to be with her, to feel her blending into him, to hold her and to have her.

He smiled at her, kissing her eyelids; he slipped

his arm beneath her hips, drawing her close to him. He moved between her legs. She gasped when she felt the pressure of his body against hers, and he stopped. "Does it hurt, love?" he inquired with quick concern, touching her cheek.

Stacey shook her head, blinking back tears that were from a source other than he imagined. The hurt was in wanting more than she could have, in seeing the limits before them that were the borders of reality. Jon was leaving. And she did not know what would happen next. "No," she whispered, and wrapped her arms around him.

"Would you tell me if it did?" But his voice was breathless, his heart was thumping, and a flush of fire consumed him as he responded to the pressure of her hands on the small of his back. He eased himself into her.

"No," she whispered, and she twined her legs with his as he sank deeply into her, holding her tightly, inhaling the fragrance of her. He wanted to sleep with her like this all night. He wanted to stay like this forever. He wanted to tell her he loved her.

But he couldn't.

It wasn't working. Jon called her every night and sometimes during the day, but it somehow wasn't enough. They talked about inconsequential things and never said much. Sometimes he thought he just wanted to hear the sound of her voice. Two weeks of steadily encroaching distance had passed, and telephone wires did not close the miles between them that were as much in his head as in fact. He had thought that once he got back to work it would all be different, that somehow this emptiness would disappear. But it didn't. The only time Stacey was completely out of his mind was when he was dancing, and, then, in some strange way he almost felt as though he was doing it for her. He could imagine her in the audience and then he could relax. He could know that she was as near as the telephone, and that allowed him to concentrate. But lately, more and more, it wasn't enough. He felt the urge to call her not once or twice but five and ten times a day. It was a dangerous addiction, and one he couldn't afford. It was frustrating to keep turning away from the telephone, but he made himself do it. He was afraid she would soon grow tired of the sound of his voice.

Stacey lived for the sound of his voice. If the telephone rang twenty times a day she would run to it each time, knowing that eventually it would be Jon. And, eventually, it always was. But the anticipation, the yearning, and the uncertainty were tearing her apart. The speeding happiness that came with his first hello faded too soon into a dull emptiness, and she did not know how much longer this could go on. They didn't seem to know what to say to each other anymore. Their separate lives were slipping between them. She couldn't help picturing him in a crowded backstage dressing room or in the hazy surroundings of his own apartment, and she felt alienated from him then, not belonging, not knowing how to breach the gap. They were worlds apart.

What did Jon want from her? Only what he had always wanted. Her friendship, her reassurance, her presence. And she wanted so much more from him, things she had no right to ask, things that were impossible for him to give. She wanted him beside her, always there for her. She wanted him to belong to her exclusively, to share neither his heart nor his body with any other woman. She wanted him, somehow, to materialize, real and solid, in her world and to stay there forever, and, of course, that was impossible. She wanted him to love her, she wanted to be free to love him. She did not know how much longer she could survive this, being torn in conflicting directions between what she dreamed for and what was possible.

Her heart leaped, as always, as she heard his voice, modified and depersonalized by the telephone receiver, greeting her cheerfully with, "Guess what?"

And then the lurching joy in her throat turned to an aching knot of no definable origin, and she found it hard to smile, even over the telephone. He was so far away. She could not touch him, in spirit or in fact. "I give up. What?"

"I'm in Boston. We're filming a show here for public television." Jon's voice was casual, though every muscle in his body was knotted. He had not mentioned this to her before because he was afraid she would not be pleased with his plans. He did not tell her now that every resource at his command had been employed to secure this deal and hasten its production, all for the sake of a few days within a hundred-mile radius of her. Would she be happy? Would she want to see him? Or would she sense the truth—that he was only using her again. "I thought we could use the time to see each other." That sounded clumsy. "That we could spend some time together while I'm here."

Did he imagine the slight hesitance on her end of the line? He hated to work before cameras; he hated this interruption in the rehearsal schedule. Yet he had played tyrant over the entire company for the past two weeks, even threatening to impress them with an artistic temper tantrum, the likes of which had never been seen before, all for the chance that she might not even want to see him. He was terrified that she might not want to see him. His hand tightened painfully on the receiver.

"That's terrific." There was pleasure in her voice, but it might have been a little hollow. Her heart was thumping. To be with him again, to see him. Would she spend the rest of her life snatching little bits and pieces of his time, being grateful for glimpses of his presence, while she watched her dreams slip through her fingers? She could not go on like this. "Why didn't you tell me before?"

Jon started breathing again. "I wasn't sure it would come through, and I wanted to surprise you. Listen, if you could drive in this afternoon—"

Something elemental in her shrank from that. To go to him, to invade his territory with her very ordinary presence—she didn't want to do that.

"I—I'm not sure, Jonathon, it's such a long drive, and I don't like to leave Mimi."

"No problem." At least she hadn't refused to see him. And he wasn't going to give her a chance to. "I could drive out to your place tonight after we finish filming, probably about five. And if you change your mind and would like to come in and watch, I'll leave a pass for you at the studio." He quickly gave her directions and finished with, "I'll see you tonight, one way or another. Let's go out for pizza, okay?"

She laughed, and he relaxed a little as he hung up the phone.

Stacey was disturbed, nervous, anxious, and a little reluctant as she thought about seeing him. Would it be different? He had been with his own kind for two weeks now, content and secure in his own world; what could he possibly want here? Even over the telephone he sounded different, as though he was no longer sure what to say to her. The time he had spent with her had been a change of pace for him, a contrast, and it was imbued with its own kind of magic for that reason. Now he might see her differently. Now he did not need her any more.

Mimi wanted to know why Stacey did not go to Boston as Jon had invited her to. "Good Lord, girl, do you realize how exhausted the man is going to be if he drives out here tonight? And then gets up and goes back in the morning? What are you thinking of?"

Stacey had not thought at all. "I just wasn't sure he really wanted me there," she hedged. "I wouldn't belong. I wouldn't know what to do."

"He wouldn't have asked you to come if he didn't want you," replied Mimi sensibly. "The only reasonable thing for you to do is stay in Boston while he's here. You can't expect him to ride that motorcycle all that way just to see you."

"He has a car, too," Stacey evaded.

And then Mimi cornered her. "Tell me something, Stacey," she demanded seriously. "Do you love Jon?"

Love. What a complicated word. It meant so many things to different people. She sighed, and no longer tried to avoid the issue. "I love him," she told her grandmother. "I loved him before I even knew him, and I love him now, but don't you see it's not"—she struggled for the words—"not real. Permanent. We live in two different worlds; we don't have anything concrete in common, and it's not the kind of love you can make a lifetime out of. It's a little bit of hero-worship, maybe. A lot of fantasy on both our parts," she admitted. "The things we give to each other, and take from each other—" She spoke slowly, putting into words her private knowledge for the first time. And it hurt. "—they're just wish-fulfillment. They aren't lasting." And at last she admitted the painful truth, the ultimate reason for the failure of her marriage. Both Stacey and her husband had counted on a fantasy to support their relationship, and the foundation just hadn't been strong enough. "It's a lot like it was with Jeff," she said quietly.

Mimi looked at her for a very long time. When

she spoke her voice was firm and her manner clear and uncompromising. "Can you see yourself growing old with Jon?" she asked simply. Registering the surprised confusion in Stacey's eyes she went on smoothly, "Will you mind if he grows bald and fat and irritable with age; will you care if he watches while your breasts sag and your thighs turn to flab and your pretty young face begins to look like a road map to China? Can you picture that, Stacey, and imagine what would keep you apart then?"

Stacey smiled. She couldn't help it. And her smile was soft and reflective, amused and tender. It was true. Of all the people in the world, she could picture herself growing old with Jon. Jon, who knew her so well, who saw beyond the exterior and into her soul, as she did with him. She could really imagine it, and there was delicate wonder in the image.

Mimi returned her smile with confidence and approval. "That's real," she said. "That's solid. And fifty years from now it won't matter whose world you live in as long as you're together. It's just an awful lot of trouble, sometimes, to get to that point. Sometimes you have to take a few chances along the way."

Stacey did not know why she went. What difference did it make if she could envision herself growing old with Jon, if she wanted to spend the rest of her life with him, growing and changing and sharing with him? What she wanted did not matter. She never should have come. She should have waited and let him come to her, safe and secure in the roles they had already built for one another. She shouldn't have threatened the status quo. That was all she could count on.

The feeling of dread grew, and even before she reached the studio she knew she had made a mistake. What was she trying to prove? Did she think this would show Jon that she wasn't afraid to meet him on his own territory, or was she trying to prove to herself that she had the courage to face whatever life offered? But she didn't. She didn't have the courage at all.

True to his word, Jon had left a pass for her. That turned the small knot of anxiety in her stomach to hope and as Stacey followed the guard down unfamiliar corridors she tried not to feel too out of place, too bedazzled and clumsy. The little red light over the door was off, and she was gestured inside into the alien world of television fantasy, unlike anything Stacey had ever known before.

The tangle of cables and cameras was confusing. The men and women who scurried around with clipboards and headsets trailing wires, shouting orders, and talking television lingo, made Stacey feel awkward and in the way as she smiled vaguely and tried to make herself invisible. In the cleared area against the abstract backdrop Stacey remembered from the live performance, dancers were rehearsing and warming up, a colorful confusion of soundless, arrhythmic dance. And there was Jon, the center of all the cacaphony, but apart from it, immersed in his own concentration as he bent over Margie in a graceful step from the pas de deux.

He was magnificent, even without the props of music and lighting. This was his world of color and grace, of unlimited imagination and boundless romance. Stacey's heart ached with love and pride as she watched him, worshiping the beauty of his movement and his command over the art—the graceful tours and the flying jetés—every line of his body in perfect symmetry, brilliant hair whirling around his head, his face an intense, self-absorbed mask of his role. It took her breath away, he was so perfect. She watched him and felt herself being captured by his spell, yet a part of her stood aside and observed it all sadly because she knew why she had come.

The morning had gone well. The scene they had shot before lunch had been accomplished in one take, to Jon's great relief. It was hard enough to divide a ballet up into scenes and shootings and to perform on command for the camera without having the additional aggravation of repeat takes. The rehearsals and warm-ups were going smoothly, and everyone was beginning to relax in the unfamiliar environment, which boded well for a productive day's work. Jon felt almost embarrassed over the early morning phone call to Stacey, as his confidence grew and his nervousness vanished. Just as always, everything was fine when he was working. He only imagined the loneliness and the need for her he felt at other times. Jon was disappointed that she hadn't come, but because he had not really expected her to, he was not greatly hurt. He would see Stacey tonight, when he needed her most, but now he had his work to take his mind off her. There was comfort in knowing that he could divide his life into two neat compartments: the one filled with dance when Stacey was not around, the other filled with her when the pressures and the emptiness became too great. It gave him hope that something could be worked out after all, and there was no need for all of this senseless suffering.

Then he looked up and saw Stacey standing there, and the relief, the joy, and the amazement that shot through him caught him completely off guard. His face lit up and he broke the routine, leaving Margie staring curiously after him as he ran over to Stacey.

"You came!" he exclaimed, catching her hands. It was unexpected, the joy he felt at seeing her. If she looked a little out of place in her cotton sundress and low-heeled sandals amid all the glitter and glamour, he pushed the knowledge to the back of his mind, squeezing her hands so hard that she winced a little. He laughed and released the pressure on her fingers, but only a fraction. He had the strangest feeling that she might disappear if he let her go. "And just in time for coffee, too," he added, slipping his arm around her shoulders and clamping down tightly. "At least, coffee for you, juice for me. Was the drive very bad?"

She glanced nervously over her shoulder as he started to lead her away. "I don't want to interrupt."

"There's plenty of time," Jon dismissed it lightly, and then a passing crewman shouted, "We're ready to roll, Jon." Jon scowled.

Stacey pulled away, her smile understanding, though still reserved. "I'll wait," she assured him.

Jon felt a low and indefinable disturbance stir. He had an irrational feeling that she wouldn't wait, that what needed to be settled between them had been postponed too long, and that if he turned his back she would walk out. He guided her toward the coffee maker, but Stacey took one look at the brightly costumed, slinky women and half naked men who lounged around it and she shook her head. Jon led her a few steps away, into a niche that was guarded by the false privacy of a collection of dusty props, and he tried to relax, smiling at her. "It's good to see you," he said softly.

He was wearing his "Fire" costume, flame-red tights with a brilliant gold sash, his torso bare. Stacey's hands ached to touch his chest, to slip her arms beneath his, and to caress his shoulders, to draw him to her one more time. She had known it all along, she had just had to prove it to herself. He was beautiful, perfect, all she had ever dreamed and more. But he did not belong to her.

He was saying, "Do you want to stay in town tonight, or drive back home?" Home. Since when had he started thinking of her house as home?

Jon's voice was light and casual, but there was anxiety in his face as he searched hers, as though he already sensed the decision she had reached so quietly and so tragically only moments before.

She was glad she had come. She had needed to see him and to see him here, to prove to herself that what she feared was a fact. He went on, "We could have dinner at the Black Ox, if you like."

And then he stopped. There was an impatient call from the crewman behind him, and lights and noise in the background as props were moved and camera angles set up for another take. Time was running out and deadlines were pushing at him. The reluctance and the sadness he saw in her eyes frightened him and he refused to read it. He tried desperately to postpone the decision he saw in her face.

He caught her face lightly between his hands, her silky hair brushing at his fingers as he leaned forward to kiss her cheek tenderly. He tried to smile. "Ah, Stacey," he sighed. "This is a mess."

She nodded soberly and spoke lowly through the knot in her throat, "I know."

Desperately he searched her eyes, hoping for some sign of reassurance there. He found none. He had a feeling that something terrible was about to happen. He tried to resign himself to it. "I've missed you," he said haltingly.

Stacey nodded, feeling a strange sense of peace flow over her, now that the moment was here. Peace, and courage to do what must be done for his sake and hers. "I've missed you, too," she said. And very far in the back of her mind she wondered calmly and sadly how she had ever imagined anything was possible between them. Jon belonged here in this world of fantasy, of illusion, chasing his dreams and making them come true for himself and for the audience who loved him. Stacey had lived too long in the world of dreams. It was time for her to grow up and face the facts. He read the truth of it in her eyes even as she said gently, "It's not fair to either of us, Jonathon." She took a breath, and she would never know afterward how she found the courage. Her voice sounded so calm, so final. "I guess," she said softly, "I've really come to say good-bye."

It stabbed at him even as he felt a slow acceptance spread over him; a burden lifted, a sense of the inevitable. He had known it all along. He had known it couldn't last, and that was what had been tearing at him these past weeks. He could not go on living two lives, torn with guilt over what he could not offer her, trying to escape the reality of her within the shelter of his work. She made demands simply by her presence, without meaning to, and they were demands he could not meet. It was better this way. She had freed him, yet some dim instinct for self-torture fought it. He said, letting his hands trail slowly to her shoulders, "It doesn't have to be this way. We can still—" he was going to say something totally inane like "be friends." He was glad she saved him from that.

She shook her head. Her eyes looked so quiet and vulnerable and strong. "There's too much emotion involved now," she said simply. "Too much wishing. We're living in limbo between the lives we wish we had and the lives we're stuck with. I'll always love you, Jonathon." And there her voice almost broke. She saved it bravely. "But you belong to a greater calling, and I have to stop living in a dream world."

He looked at her for a long time, not knowing what to say. He heard his name shouted again. He knew it was best; he knew she was right. What could he offer her? Life on the road, pieces of his time, with her doing all the giving and him doing all the receiving. Stacey needed solidity and security and a basis in permanence. She needed love. At last the best he could come up with was, "I never meant to hurt you."

She even managed a vague, unconvincing smile. "That's part of life, isn't it?" But then, quietly, sincerely, "I'm not sorry."

From behind him again, threateningly, "Callan! This is costing us money!"

He looked distractedly over his shoulder. He didn't want to leave it like this. Someone grabbed his arm. He said a little desperately, shrugging off the touch, "I'll call you."

And then came the hardest thing Stacey had ever had to do. She shook her head. "Better not," she said.

Jon looked at her in sorrow and despair, but there was nothing he could do but understand. The hand was tugging at his arm again.

"Be great!" she called after him, and he thought he saw a shimmer of tears in her eyes, behind her smile, just before he turned away.

Bright lights flooded him; positions were taken. It was best. What else could she have done? She had suffered through a make-believe marriage; he had told her himself she was only using him for escape. He should be proud of her, that she had found the courage to admit the truth to herself. He should be grateful to her for freeing him from obligations he could not fulfill. He, too, had had his escape in her; he had had his chance to live two lives and had discovered indisputably that it could not work. He could not be torn between commitments, and he could not ask her to live with him without one. No, it was best this way. He was back where he belonged, and he wouldn't regret it. He had made his choice, and there was no chance for reconsideration.

The music swelled. The cameras were rolling. Jon was into the first steps of a mystical tale of magic.

Stacey was gone. It hit him suddenly and without warning, the truth of it. She didn't want him to call. She didn't want to see him, ever. She would not be there for him anymore.

His heart was pounding, and the powerful music was only dim background noise. What else could he have expected? He was not a complete fool; he must have known all along that it would end this way.

He wasn't concentrating. He had lost the tempo and Margie was giving him a shocked, incredulous look. The director shouted, "Cut!" and Jon was startled. The other dancers looked embarrassed as they moved back to their original positions, and Jon felt a hot wave of humiliation and confusion creep over him. *He* had been the cause of an interrupted production? He had never done anything like that before. He gave a nervous, abashed grin and smoothed his damp palms on his tights. The director smiled encouragingly at him. *All right, concentrate.* The cameras were rolling again.

Was there anything he could have done? Stacey couldn't expect him to divide himself between two great loves. He had told her from the beginning his choice was made, and all the rest was just make-believe. Fifth position, plié; six steps, tour—or was it tour jeté. *Damn it, concentrate.* Perspiration was gathering in his armpits and trickling down his sides. His heart was thundering, and around him red and gold and blue veils whirled like a scene from a nightmare, fast and faster, obscuring the borders of reality and leaving him behind.

There must be a compromise somewhere. Jon was sure of it. There was a way they could work it out; there was no law that said he must sacrifice Stacey for his work. It was not carved in stone that an artist must suffer for greatness. He did not want to suffer. He wanted—

Forget it. Forget her. This was real and present, this was where he belonged. She had come into his life and only brushed it; she was part of the past and could not threaten him now, for he still had his work, his one great calling.

The music was like a raucous blur in his ears as he waited, kneeling on the stage, for his next solo. His next solo. He had gotten along fine without her before, and he would do so now. No, he had not gotten along fine, he had waited all his life for her. And why did the future look so empty without her? Never to hear Stacey's voice again, never to see the quick understanding in her eyes, never to feel the comfort of her arms—he was dramatizing. He would get over it. He was back where he belonged.

He almost missed his cue. *Damn*. What was happening to him? He had been nervous before, but now he was terrified. Once he was onstage and caught up in the mystery of a performance everything was always all right. Perspiration was streaming from his hair and sheening his body, but he felt cold. He had performed this routine a dozen times, a hundred, he had choreographed it, but now he couldn't remember the steps. The lights were pinning him to his humiliation, the cameras capturing his defeat; it was every nightmare come true. He could not hear the music for the thundering of his heart. He couldn't see where he was supposed to be for the madly whirling bodies before him. There seemed to be accusation and derision in every face. You should have stopped her, you fool. You should have given her what she needed. You should have loved her. What was it Mimi had said? Love is a commitment that allows no options. Take it or leave it. But once you take it—

It was a choice. There was no compromise. Love requires a decision, an effort, a dedication, just like the dance. And Jon had avoided too long making that decision.

He had to concentrate. He was going to ruin the performance. He couldn't concentrate. *All right, then, fake it*. And then he saw Stacey.

Stacey saw the fall. She knew that she should have left, but the moment Jon walked away from her all her courage deserted her; she could only stand there and watch him, one last time, watch him through hot, blurry eyes and with a knot of agony that was threatening to smother her.

Stacey knew he was upset. She shouldn't have done this to him before a performance. She saw him break the routine, and she was horrified that she had done that to him. She knew how he feared rejection. She had no right to come here, to do this to him before a performance.

She was turning away, knowing she had to leave, to get out of his life while she still could, and out of the corner of her eye she saw him fall. She heard his cry, though whether it was of pain or shock she did not know, and at that moment it did not matter. Everything was frozen around her. The other dancers, the technicians, were all motionless, stunned, horrified. No one, nothing, moved, and Stacey stood there with a cold spear of agony rising upward in her throat that felt like a silent scream as she simply stared. Jon Callan—perfect, invincible, immortal—had fallen. She could not believe it.

Abruptly the taped music was cut off. As though the threads that bound them to incredulity and shock were suddenly snapped, everyone began to move at once, shouting orders, rushing toward Jon. And Stacey was among them, running, pushing her way through unfamiliar bodies, trying not to sob out loud until she knelt beside Jon.

Someone was shouting, "Call an ambulance!"

Another cried, "Oh, it's broken, I know it is." And other voices, calmer, though just as frightened, advised him to be still, asked him how bad it was, hovered over him and tried to reassure him, and murmured meaningless phrases of helpless concern. Stacey knew he would not want her to see him. He would not want her to witness his failure, his humiliation. But she knelt beside him and took his hand and he turned to look at her.

Jon's face was white and wet; his eyes were dark with shock, and then quickly went darker and wider when he saw her. Then swiftly, before she could register the change of expression on his face, his arms were around her, crushing her, holding her as she held him, whispering tightly, "Oh, Stacey, I'm so glad you didn't leave. So glad."

What happened next was such a confusion of motion and emotions, shouts and voices and actions that afterward Stacey would never remember the details of it clearly. She remembered the tight squeeze of Jon's fingers on hers as he was carried to his dressing room, the look of bright wonder in his eyes, the way he wouldn't let her leave, even when the doctor examined him. And then there were just the two of them, hours or minutes later, alone in the dressing room, and the quietness and peace that surrounded them was almost as much of a shock as the chaos that had gone before.

Jon was lying on the blue divan in his robe, his bandaged ankle propped up on two pillows, his eyes closed wearily. His ankle was not broken, just twisted. Stacey knelt on the floor beside him, her fingers captured in his, and still muffled waves of shock were pounding her. Still she could not believe it. Jon Callan of mystique and magic, the man who made dreams come true, infallible—but human. With human frailties and vulnerabilities. There was wonder and there was shock. He was not perfect. He sometimes made mistakes. But he was real, and human.

She stroked his damp hair with trembling fingers. "Jonathon," she whispered, "I'm so sorry."

He opened his eyes. There was a hint of a smile there. "I'm not," he said simply. "That fall woke me up. It was long overdue."

She stared at him, not understanding, almost afraid to imagine what he meant. He sat up, wincing a little as he shifted the position of his foot, warding off her automatic protective gesture. He exerted a small pressure on her hand and drew her to sit beside him. She did not understand that calm, contented look on his face or the smile that seemed to reach out to her and pull her heart to his. It was all happening too fast, she could not follow it. She said with deep, anxious concern, "Does it hurt much?"

"Like hell," he shrugged cheerfully. "Ego and ankle. But," he told her seriously, "it's probably the best thing that could have happened to me. I think everyone needs to face his worst nightmare at least once, just to get a good look at reality."

And Stacey's worst nightmare had come true the moment she had heard him cry out, the moment she had known he was hurt. She suffered with him. She could not help it. She loved him so much.

He held both of her hands in a calm, warm clasp, and his eyes soothed her, reassuring her, speaking to her of things that were real and forever. "Something happened to me on that stage today, Stacey," he said quietly. "It's something I never dreamed was possible before. I always thought the art was what mattered, it was the only sure and lasting thing in my life, the only thing I could dedicate myself to completely. I thought there wasn't room for anything else. But today I found out that, whether I liked it or not, you had crept into every part of my life and that without you nothing else made sense. I couldn't separate you from what I did on stage; I couldn't live two lives any longer. Because, guess what?" He touched her cheek lightly, his eyes catching the wonder of a new and deep emotion. His lips blurred into a tender smile and he said softly, "I love you. The old-fashioned to-have-and-to-hold kind, till death do us part, the real thing. I simply can't help it, Stacey. You are all of me, and nothing else matters without you."

Stacey had stopped breathing, but she felt the rush of joy and life surge into her lungs as he drew her into his arms, hesitantly at first, as though almost afraid she would reject him, and then tightly, powerfully, as her arms went around him and she pressed him close. For he was all of her, too; she had known it always, known that a part of her would forever be with him, but now he was real. Now she was no longer afraid, because they could share all that life presented to them together—dreams and heartaches, good times and bad, uncertainties and triumphs—forever.

She could feel the rush of his breath against her ear, the thumping of his heart. There was urgency in his embrace and in his words, as though he was still half-anxious that if he gave her a chance she would disappear. "I know I have no right to disrupt your life, Stacey," he whispered. "I can't ask you to give up your home and your career for the crazy life we lead on the road. But it's all right," he said quickly, and he meant it. He had never meant anything more sincerely. All he wanted to do was to give to her, whatever it took. He pushed her away a little, looking at her. "I'll take the position with the Boston Ballet. We can live here and have a quiet, normal life—kids and rose gardens and all the things you're used to."

Stacey smiled at him through a sudden film of tears of wonder and happiness and gratitude. "I'll make a deal with you," she said, smoothing back the dampened strand of hair that still clung to his forehead. "I'll give you two years on the road, and when you get your own company with your own backers and your own style, you give me twenty years of kids and rose gardens—all the things we both want."

Jon had never felt so intensely, never loved so much, never felt the soaring freedom of happiness that seemed at that moment to transport him to another world. But he teased, "Only twenty?"

"Thirty, then," she conceded, and moved back

into his arms. "Or forty." She felt his lips descend upon hers.

He held her, his arms tightening until a tremor within them mirrored the depth of his emotion. Then, ever so slightly, he let the muscles relax. "It's not going to be easy, Stacey," he said quietly. "It's something we have to work at and practice every day—just like dancing." His eyes, fixed now upon hers, were sober. "Happily ever after is only in fairy stories, you know. Loving each other in the real world is more a matter of trying than magic."

Stacey smiled, quietly and with gentle confidence. "But it's the trying that keeps the magic alive," she said.

Jon released a breath of loving agreement and pulled her once again into his arms.

A long time later Jon murmured contentedly into her hair, "See, this was a lucky accident. A twisted ankle is going to keep me offstage for a few weeks"—he bent to brush her lips with his own, his eyes alive with pleasure—"but it should in no way interfere with the things people normally do on a honeymoon."

Stacey's eyes sparkled and danced invitingly back at him. "Is that a promise?"

"Only the first of many," he assured her, and sought her lips again briefly, playfully. "You won't mind," he challenged lightly, "holding my hand when I get scared and telling me how wonderful I am when I'm down and watching my diet?"

Stacey hugged him. "Better yet," she promised, her eyes glowing. "I'll let you get fat when you're forty, and I won't even mind."

Resting against him, holding him, content with the promise of many more delights to come, Stacey laughed softly. "Mimi is going to love this," she answered his questioning look. "Now she can finally sell her house and move to that retirement home. I'm off her conscience."

Jon squeezed her briefly, nuzzling her neck. "Can we go home now and tell her?"

Stacey moved away from him, smiling tenderly, loving him abundantly. She cupped his face with her hands; she kissed his cheek. "Yes," she said. "Let's go home."

Enter a uniquely exciting new world with

Harlequin American Romance™

Harlequin American Romances are the first romances to explore today's love relationships. These compelling novels reach into the hearts and minds of women across America... probing the most intimate moments of romance, love and desire.

You'll follow romantic heroines and irresistible men as they boldly face confusing choices. Career first, love later? Love without marriage? Long-distance relationships? All the experiences that make love real are captured in the tender, loving pages of **Harlequin American Romances.**

What makes American women so different when it comes to love? Find out with **Harlequin American Romance!**

Send for your introductory FREE book now!

Get this book FREE!

Mail to:

Harlequin Reader Service

In the U.S.
2504 West Southern Ave.
Tempe, AZ 85282

In Canada
P.O. Box 2800, Postal Station A
5170 Yonge St., Willowdale, Ont. M2N 6J3

YES! I want to be one of the first to discover
Harlequin American Romance. Send me FREE and without
obligation *Twice in a Lifetime.* If you do not hear from me after I
have examined my FREE book, please send me the 4 new
Harlequin American Romances each month as soon as they
come off the presses. I understand that I will be billed only $2.25
for each book (total $9.00). There are no shipping or handling
charges. There is no minimum number of books that I have to
purchase. In fact, I may cancel this arrangement at any time.
Twice in a Lifetime is mine to keep as a FREE gift, even if I do not
buy any additional books.   154-BPA-NAXP

Name   (please print)

Address   Apt. no.

City   State/Prov.   Zip/Postal Code

Signature (If under 18, parent or guardian must sign.)